# A Moment in Time

# A Moment in Time

*A Journey of Faith, Hope, and Love*

MARY S. HANSON

iUniverse, Inc.
New York   Bloomington

*A Moment In Time*
*A Journey of Faith, Hope, and Love*

*Copyright © 2009 by Mary S. Hanson*

*Disclaimer: The views expressed in this work are solely those of the author and do not necessarily reflect the views of the publisher, and the publisher hereby disclaims any responsibility for them. The names of rehabilitation facilities have been changed to protect privacy.*

*iUniverse books may be ordered through booksellers or by contacting:*

*iUniverse*
*1663 Liberty Drive*
*Bloomington, IN 47403*
*www.iuniverse.com*
*1-800-Authors (1-800-288-4677)*

*Because of the dynamic nature of the Internet, any Web addresses or links contained in this book may have changed since publication and may no longer be valid.*

*ISBN: 978-1-4401-2185-2 (pbk)*
*ISBN: 978-1-4401-2186-9 (ebk)*

*Library of Congress Control Number: 2009923909*

*Printed in the United States of America*

*iUniverse Rev. 8/26/09*

# DEDICATION

This book is dedicated to all of the people who prayed for our daughter; to her friends who stood by her with the hope and enthusiasm that only youth can exhibit; to our neighbors and co-workers who nourished not only our bodies but our souls; to the many people who called and wrote letters of support without expecting anything in return; to the doctors and nurses and therapists who used their God-given gifts to treat our daughter skillfully and aggressively; to the staff and students at Bell Middle School for their endless supply of hugs and kind deeds; to the staff at Dousman Elementary School for remembering one of their own and for keeping her spirit alive; to our minister for keeping us focused; to my husband for his eternal wisdom; to our boys for never giving up; and

**to my daughter Laura, who, at every stage of her life, has taught me the true meaning of LOVE.**

# FOREWORD

In one moment in time, our lives can change forever. Mary Hanson's spiritual journey, following one of *these* moments, transports you out of the day-to-day superficiality of life into the depths of your own vulnerability, where you will struggle with the *real issues of life*. When you have finished reading, you will feel like a soldier returning from war, trying to understand why people are so focused on the things that don't really matter, and wondering why we waste so much energy on them instead of making each moment count and loving each other and our God above all else.

*A Moment in Time* is the story of Mary's beloved daughter Laura, who suffered a traumatic brain injury in an automobile accident. It is a journal of the gut wrenching days, weeks, months, and years that followed. Hang on to your heartstrings, because you're about to take a ride into a world of shattered dreams and crosses borne. I am an avid reader, and I have never read anything as raw as this account.

As Mary's parish nurse, I was a bystander, but without this book, I could have never known the depth of her experience. As she exposes her deepest thoughts and feelings throughout this wonderfully real disclosure of her family's painful struggle, you have no choice but to go there, too. This is a real story about a real family on a very real faith journey.

Mary asks the questions most of us aren't brave enough to ask. None of us is exempt from sorrow. If you want guidance, encouragement, hope, and support for your journey, this is it. Those who have said, "I can't do this," but did it because they had no choice, will learn how to reach deeper into themselves. Mary writes, "It is rising above tragedy that defines the human spirit and distinguishes us from the circumstances in which we find ourselves. It is, in the end, what connects us with the God we are seeking."

In this journey, Mary tries over and over to find security in insecure comforts and material pleasures, seeking the same satisfaction as before her daughter's accident, only to discover the value has diminished. You will want to glean the wisdom that is woven throughout this book. Come along and experience a powerful story of advocacy, of a family fighting on behalf of someone they love more than themselves, in the midst of a healthcare system that gives up on them.

As a healthcare professional, I gained a new perspective from Mary's story. I saw that our profession has become consumed with its own expertise rather than actually helping! We, as healthcare workers, have been so hard pressed to keep up with a changing system that we may have become insensitive and unaware of our inability to really understand. We unintentionally convey a lack of vision and give up on people without the perseverance and perspective that their loved ones keep as they hold on to the person that we never had the chance to know.

As you watch each family member cope with the same pain in different ways, you will gain insight into the task they face as they are forced to let go of the loved one they knew and get to know the person she is becoming. You will see the power to overcome, when love, prayer, and action are combined. You will see the value of journaling your way through unbearable circumstances. You will definitely be challenged to ponder thoughts like: "Must we know despair to become wise?" or, "So many parents are concerned about providing their children with everything, but they neglect the quiet places of the heart, the place where children learn to have faith, hope, love, and a belief in a power greater than themselves, which will allow them to withstand the circumstances of their lives."

As a fellow pilgrim on this spiritual journey with this awesome family, my faith has been challenged and reevaluated several times. This work is compelling, not only because of what you will learn about the Hansons, but also because of what you will learn about brain injury, and ultimately, what you will learn about yourself.

One of the greatest gifts of this story is that it has no visible resolution. This story will force you to think about how to find joy and live day to day with experiences that continue to bring a chronic level of pain indefinitely. Mary is right when she writes that the soul will triumph over the most difficult circumstances.

This is the best account I've ever read about letting go of the life you planned, so as to live the life that is waiting for you; letting go of old dreams and old identities so that you can become all that God created you to be; and discovering a life that is deeper and richer and more alive than ever before.

After reading this gripping account, you will want to reassess your values and priorities and grab on to each moment with those you love. You will wonder how people without faith survive at all, or why they would ever want to.

Sue Konkel, Parish Nurse<br>
Oconomowoc, Wisconsin

*This book is a series of thoughts, fragmented by time, connected only by the passion which binds us to our dreams and our memories. It flows like sand through our fingers. We clench desperately to hold on to what is good, only to find the moments of our lives washed away by the tide of times. Like the tiny grains of sand, each moment is as important as the next, and yet infinitesimal in the greater scheme of events.*

—Mary Hanson

# MY DAUGHTER, MY LOVE, MY BEST FRIEND

*Mom,*

*I've been meaning to write to you, but I guess my time has been limited with my new RA job. I wanted to let you know how special a mother you truly are. A few weeks ago, I was packing for school, and I came across the book you put together for graduation. I started crying reading it and realized how lucky I was, not only to have the best mother, but the best friend anyone could ever ask for. Your strength, energy, heart, and kindness encourage me to be the best I can be at all times! I don't know why I was selected to be the luckiest girl in the whole world, but I am thankful that I was. You truly are a blessing, Mother, and I love you to pieces. God bless. Thanks, Mom, for being my mom. Miss you lots.*

*Love ya,*
*Laura*

This is the last letter I received from my daughter. On October 23, 1998, she was returning to school from a hayride when her car hit a patch of gravel and struck a tree. She was flown by Flight for Life helicopter to Froedtert Hospital where she remains in a coma today. I don't know if she'll ever wake up, or, if she does, whether she'll ever be the same. I do know that I'll always be there for her, and she'll always be my best friend. In her nineteen years, she has taught me, and so many others she has met, so much about how to live. By her example, she has taught us to love more, pray harder, and worry less. She has taught us to live life to the fullest—every minute, every hour, every day.

Right now we're praying for a miracle; and I believe in miracles! Whatever detour God has planned for her life, she will always be close to my heart. My daughter's letter is not about me. It is a reflection of what lies behind her closed eyes: *her* strength, *her* energy, *her* heart, *her* kindness, *her* love for people, for life, and for God.

My daughter has always wanted to be a teacher ever since I can remember. I know that if she were here right now, she would look across the room and smile—the most infectious, heartwarming smile you could ever imagine—and she would ask, "How can I help you?" And so, I look across the room at all of these bright young faces, so eager, so full of promise, and gather all the strength I have to smile and ask, "How can I help you?" and go on ...

(Metropolitan Milwaukee's Young Authors Conference;
November 1998)

# I

I'm not going to start with the dreams I had for my daughter—
of getting married, having children, and becoming a teacher.
All mothers have those dreams. I'm going to begin instead with
the night all of those dreams were shattered, the night of my
daughter's accident, when, in one moment in time, her life, and
the lives of every member of our family changed forever.

It was a Friday. My husband and I were exhausted from
the week. Our youngest son Justin had just completed football
season. Jaime, our oldest, was on his own and had a good job.
Laura was in college, and life was beginning to slow down a bit. It
was still a hectic fall, much of it our own making. We had joked
about keeping the car running, taking Justin to band practice,
piano lessons, orthodontic appointments, and confirmation
classes. It was a good life, but we were looking forward to a quiet
weekend.

Laura was at the Kettle Moraine Ranch. She was the
resident assistant for her dorm and had organized a hayride for
the students on her floor. My husband and I had fallen asleep.
An hour later we were awakened suddenly by two policemen
standing at the front door. They asked if we owned a red Toyota
Tercel. We said, "Yes." They told us that our daughter had been

in a serious accident and she had been flown by Flight for Life helicopter to Froedtert Memorial Hospital in Milwaukee. They gave us a card, wrote the address of the hospital on the back of it, and left.

Was this a dream? Would we soon wake up? We needed to get to the hospital. Our daughter needed us. I called Jaime, and he met us in the emergency room at Froedtert. We were greeted at the door by a social worker who escorted us immediately into a small private waiting room. She asked if she could get us anything, water, coffee? It was surreal. I asked for a chaplain. We waited and stared at each other in disbelief. The trauma surgeon entered the room. He explained that our daughter was in critical condition with serious head injuries. She was in a coma. He used numbers to explain her condition. On the Glasgow coma scale of zero to fifteen, she was a one. Below that she would be considered brain dead, and below that—I could not listen anymore.

Another doctor entered the room. He was a neurosurgeon. He explained to us that our daughter was going to be taken to intensive care. CAT scans indicated there was bleeding in one of the ventricles. They were going to insert a tube into her brain and drain fluid in order to allow for swelling. I asked if we could see her. They took us into the emergency room. I overheard one of the nurses say, "Shh, that's the family." My daughter was lying on a cart. Her arms stretched inward as we spoke. We assured her that we loved her and that everything would be okay. I learned later that her gestures were a sign of the seriousness of her brain injury. The doctors called it posturing. I called it *hanging on to life*.

We were then led down a seemingly endless corridor and ushered into a larger waiting room. It was dark, except for the dim lights of the distant corridor. We again waited in silence. The chaplain arrived, and we began to pray. We had no words. The chaplain guided our thoughts. We held onto each other, asking with all of our hearts for God to spare the life of our daughter.

A nurse entered the waiting room. She was comforting, but could not answer the only important question our hearts were asking: "Will Laura be all right?" She led us into the intensive care unit, which specialized in brain injuries. When we next saw our daughter, there were tubes everywhere. She was hooked up to machines monitoring her pulse, her heart rate, her blood pressure. Fluids were being pumped in and fluids were being drained out. Her head was partially shaved and her beautiful blonde hair was all matted together. A breathing tube hung out of her mouth. There was a constant beeping of monitors and shuffling of equipment as the medical staff moved quietly but vigorously to save her life.

We were again led into a small room where the neurosurgeon explained to us that the procedure to drain spinal fluid from her brain had gone well. X-rays showed that her pelvis was fractured in four places and that she had also fractured her arm. He told us to prepare for the worst and hope for the best, then go home and get a little sleep. It was 5:00 am. We were handed a bag of bloodstained clothes that had been cut off of her at the scene of the accident and told to look through them for valuables. Most people, we were told, then threw them away.

Throw them away? Valuables? How could anything be more valuable than my daughter's life? Sleep? Prepare for the worst? How does a parent do that? All of her life we've been preparing her—for school, for prom, for piano recitals, for college, for life. We didn't know how to prepare for anything but the best for our children. I took a picture of our family from my wallet and laid it on her heart. I wanted her to know that we were not far away. I also wanted the medical staff to know that this was not just another patient. This was Laura: my daughter, my love, and my best friend.

We went home, but we couldn't stay there. We made a few phone calls, cleaned up, and returned to the hospital to wait and pray. People arrived throughout the day: Hanns, Jenna, Sally—Laura's friends—the Hansons, Mark and Jean, our minister. The doctors did everything humanly possible to save Laura's life. But there was nothing they could do to save her future. That was in the hands of God, and he would let us know in time.

The next few days were a blur. She had survived the first twenty-four hours. That was a miracle. We were told that the next three to five days were critical. The brain would swell considerably during that time. Again she beat the odds. At one point, when our family was praying at her bedside, she quivered. We had never seen anything like it before or since. I knew it was a sign from God that she was responding to prayer. She was going to make it. She was going to come back to us.

More people arrived at the hospital. They prayed with us and cried with us. Many sent cards and food and did what they could to lend support. But Laura remained in a coma. We kept recreating the scene over and over, trying to make sense of what had happened, how it could possibly have happened. But it didn't make sense. Laura was in the prime of her life. She did everything right. She was concentrating on her driving. She wasn't speeding. She was just on a hayride with students from her dorm. *What if* I had called her that night? I would have told her I'd see her the next day and we'd go out to lunch together.*What if* we hadn't bought her that car? It had dual air bags and was supposed to be safe. *What if* we had started her in kindergarten a year later? She wouldn't have been an RA and organized the hayride. *What if, what if, what if, what if?* Life just doesn't seem fair. If only I could drive into that tree. But what if she wakes up and I'm not there?

The calls, the cards, the food, and the visits from friends were encouraging. But we gathered most of our strength from prayer. We felt so empty and helpless. At one point, I asked

God to use me to channel all of his strength into Laura. After all, if he could make hurricanes and tornadoes and tell a tiny spider how to weave a perfect web, he could certainly heal my daughter. I also asked for strength to accept whatever her future would be. I was not ready to accept the unacceptable—and yet, I had no choice. I knew I needed help. The following Sunday, our minister said, "If you're looking for Jesus, don't look up, look across." I did, and I found him everywhere.

I thought about the articles that I had written about religion shortly before the accident. For most of my life, God had been an intellectual exercise, and religion was simply a matter of identity. Church seemed to have nothing to do with either. Now it didn't seem to make a difference whether the church took a stand on morality or whether Western religions had more substance than Eastern religions. My prayers did not use the words of any religion. They formed no concepts. They sought no answers. They were prayers for strength, for guidance, and for healing.

For ten days, Laura remained in the neurological intensive care unit (NICU). When her vital signs stabilized, she was moved to another floor. She was now breathing through a tracheotomy tube and being fed through a tube in her stomach. She was given large doses of antibiotics to counter various infections in her lungs and her bladder. One arm was in a cast; the other was black and blue from I-Vs. The metal rod inserted into her leg to pull her hip into place had been removed. They would deal with bones later.

Before leaving NICU, we had to meet with members of the neurological team in order to make arrangements for Laura's care upon dismissal from Froedtert. That was when we met Nurse Death. We were already stressed beyond belief. We hadn't slept. Meals were what appeared on our table, like manna from heaven. We were confused, disoriented, and depressed. Nurse Death entered the room with a stack of medical textbooks. On top was a picture book of the brain written for second graders. I wasn't sure which book she was planning to use. To my surprise, she used all of them. She wanted to make sure that we knew how terrible things really were. She told us that Laura's entire brain was injured, that it had been sheared from the brain stem, that damaged nerve cells could never be repaired, and that she could hang up her shingle at any time, so she knew what she was talking about. But she didn't know Laura. She didn't know that at nineteen Laura had more inner strength than most people hope to have in a lifetime. She didn't know that Laura could warm a room with just her smile, and move mountains with her personality. She didn't know that with all the love and support from her family and friends, Laura would come back. We knew. We all knew.

There were others who were more hopeful. The nurses in NICU were encouraging, but Karen helped us the most. She told us the story of a young boy who had been in a coma for five weeks. He survived and went on to live a normal life. There were deficits, but there was hope. She not only helped Laura survive that first week, she helped our family survive, too. We hung on to her every word.

On November 19, three and a half weeks after her accident, Laura's classmates from Whitewater sponsored a wheelchair basketball game in the university gym. Over eight hundred people attended. There were pictures of Laura everywhere, and banners describing her personality hung on the gym wall. There was a moment of silent prayer, then cheers for her recovery. People came to us with stories: stories of how she had the loudest room in the dorm, day and night; how her door was always open if someone needed a haircut or a manicure, or just to talk. Her teachers told us how much she was missed. She was such a spark in every class. We were overwhelmed! It is difficult to describe our feelings that night. The love and respect and admiration and support that people showed for our daughter would make any parent proud. They shared our grief. And for a moment, we shared their enthusiasm. But Laura was still in a coma, and we missed her more than ever.

The students at Whitewater had also made ribbons, blue ribbons for Laura's big blue eyes. They were distributed everywhere on campus. Our family each wore one, and it was not long before ribbons were everywhere: at work, at Justin's school. It gave us hope. Following the game, Jaime walked back to Laura's dorm room with Sally, one of Laura's good friends. Her room looked just like it had the night of the accident. Nothing had changed—yet, everything had changed. Outside her door, a crowd of students had gathered. They were starved for information about our daughter. How was she? What could they do? When would she return?

We were all grieving, just in different ways. Jerry was doing everything he could to help our family return to a *normal* life. He found diversion in teaching, watching the Packers, and dealing with the mounting legal work that resulted from the accident. He focused on keeping Justin connected—to school, to church, and to social activities. Jaime had his job as a financial analyst. He reached a level of acceptance long before the rest of us, and he was committed to helping Laura fully recover. He was no longer able to maintain a relationship with his girlfriend, however, since he was spending long hours at the hospital, and his emotional energy was becoming drained. His optimism carried us through the first four weeks of this ordeal. But the stress was taking its toll on him, and there were times when he was discouraged at the lack of progress. Justin was holding his own, and I thought many times about all that he had learned since Laura's accident: the importance of family, friends, and church; coping with stress; and living life to the fullest, one day at a time.

As for me, I was falling apart. It had been four weeks since the accident. One Friday I left school early, unable to finish the day, and drove to the hospital to be with Laura. When I finally arrived home, I was a wreck. Jerry asked me why I thought I had the only corner on grief. I couldn't answer. I didn't know what was in his heart. I could only imagine. For nineteen years, he had done everything humanly possible to guard and protect his daughter from harm. And now he was helpless. He had no control over what had happened or what will happen. He was carrying a big load, and he needed me to help lighten it. He couldn't deal with my grief on top of his.

I couldn't understand why everyone else was able to move on, and I seemed to be so stuck in time. Was it because I was Laura's mother? Was it because I had given birth to her, and she was part of me? Was it because I had nursed her so long, and I had become part of her? Or was it because I loved her and just missed her so very much? Now Laura needed me. My family needed me. I had a job to do, and it was time to move on.

# II

Laura had been in a coma for four weeks. She had been moved to Sacred Hands Rehabilitation Center, located in one of the largest hospitals on Milwaukee's east side. She was involved in an experimental coma stimulation program designed to bring her out of her coma, although there was considerable controversy over whether this was possible. Her tracheotomy tube had been removed. She was breathing on her own. Her arm was out of a cast, and physically, she appeared to be doing well. But she still did not respond to our constant pleas to open her eyes.

The following Sunday, our minister began his sermon with the story of what has since been called the *Heidi* game. This caught my husband's attention. On November 17, 1968, the New York Jets were playing the Oakland Raiders. Two minutes before the end of the game, in what seemed like a certain victory for the New York Jets, NBC interrupted the game to show the movie *Heidi*. Football fans will remember vividly what happened next. Oakland ran several touchdowns and went on to beat the New York Jets. It was an ending no one could have ever predicted.

I'm not a football fan, but I began to see where the minister was going with his sermon. We always seem to think we know where we're going in life, how things are going to end. He went on to say that *our lives are part of a larger context, and no matter what happens to us, God can transform the experience.* There is meaning to life. There is purpose. Even more importantly, behind life *there is one who can help us turn negatives into positives, tragedies into triumphs, and heartaches into hallelujahs.* None of us ever knows how things are going to end. So much of our grief is caused by anticipating the worst. I knew we were on a marathon. We would have to take one baby step at a time, and we needed to be patient.

I still couldn't imagine how something so tragic could be turned into something triumphant. Laura was so young, so beautiful, so talented. She had so much to live for and so much yet to give. How could God do this to her, to us?

Thanksgiving was particularly difficult. Yet, we were again reminded that the first Thanksgiving was celebrated not amidst abundance and plenty, but amidst desolation and disappointment. We had much for which to be thankful. Laura was still alive, and there was still hope for recovery. But what would emerge from her quiet cocoon? The daughter we had known was gone forever. Would I be able to accept her new personality, her physical deformities, her diminished mental functioning? I had never accepted less than perfection in anything. How could I begin to accept it now? What kind of future could she possibly have? Would she ever marry? Have children? Her dreams had been mingled with mine. It seemed so unfair. How does a person ever get over something like this, tragedies that happen for no reason at all? I guess no one ever does. One just moves through it, finding pleasure in momentary distractions, comfort in family and friends, and solace in God.

We found humor wherever possible. I remember a night at the hospital when we were praying at Laura's bedside with two very dear friends, when, out of the corner of my eye, I saw our two boys whiz down the hall in wheelchairs. They were trying to escape the incessant questioning of a well-meaning visitor. They continued out the door and onto the sixth floor of the parking ramp, where they raced their way down to the exit. I knew Laura would get a kick out of it, and I was anxious to tell her.

By the fifth week, Laura began to emerge from her coma. She was making slow but steady progress. She was able to hold her head erect while sitting in a wheelchair, and she was moving her right arm more. Jerry seemed content with these baby steps, but I wouldn't be satisfied until I had my daughter back.

There was some disagreement within the medical community as to when Laura actually came out of the coma. Some say it is when she first opened her eyes; others, when she began to respond to commands. Laura was beginning to show some signs of responsiveness. Her eyes would occasionally open and for longer periods of time. She began to focus. She also began to show evidence of more normal wake/sleep cycles.

More and more people began to visit her in the hospital. We kept a notebook in her room and asked visitors to record their observations. It was tremendously helpful. Since we were with her every day, the changes that we noticed were small. But people who had not seen her for longer periods of time were amazed at her progress. The notebook not only allowed people to communicate with us, it gave them the opportunity to communicate with Laura. It also let us know who had come to visit during our absence. One visitor wrote the following:

*Dear Laura,*

*This is the third time I have seen you. You are even better than the last time. When you are all back and take a look through this, you will be surprised to find out all the friends and loved ones you are*

11

*blessed with. I graduate in a few weeks (Dec. 20), and have been really caught up in just getting done. Having a goal like this helps you to lose sight of some things that can be important. How do I say thank you for bringing me closer to an appreciation of every morning and every good-bye said? You will be fine.*

*Mike*

My entry was always the same, although I never wrote it down:

*There isn't a day, an hour or a minute, Laura, that I don't think of you. I love you dearly,*

*Mom*

# III

Families who have experienced the death of a loved one move through all of the stages of grief: shock, denial, anger, and acceptance—not necessarily in any order and not all at the same time. Social and religious rituals can help families as they move through these various stages. When families encounter brain injury to a loved one, they pass through similar stages of grief, but without the rituals to help them cope. It is not clear to anyone but the family that the one they knew and loved is gone forever.

If Laura had died the night of her accident, there would have been closure. Instead, a part of me died that night, and there is no closure. It is like a nightmare from which we will never wake up. As long as there is even the slightest bit of hope that she will recover, there will never be closure for our family. And yet we needed to come to terms with what we had lost before we could fully accept what was about to unfold in our lives.

Christmas was even harder than Thanksgiving. At any moment I expected Laura to come home from college, throw her arms around us, and tell us how glad she was to be home. She had done that so many times before. We'd then go shopping together, sample all the perfumes at the cosmetic counters, and try on as many clothes as we had time for. She looked gorgeous in anything she tried on, with her long blonde hair and her beautiful blue eyes. She loved everything she touched; but when she bought something, it was usually for someone else. She had everything a girl could ever want: looks, intelligence, charm, warmth, and personality. She was the spark that always lifted our spirits, the one who was levelheaded, the one who seemed to do everything right. This just shouldn't have happened to her. But it did.

Laura was always there for everyone. When she first met her residents at the dorm, she told them that her door was always open, day or night, just to talk; and it was. She was there for Jaime, particularly as she grew older and became more of a friend than a little sister. She was especially there for Justin. Since the day he was born, she had been his other mom and my little helper. She would play with him for hours on end, in the sand at our summer home on Washington Island, and in the basement where she had set up school. He was her student, and she helped him learn to read. She was there for him nearly every night until she went to college, to take him to soccer practice, to feed him snacks, or just to talk. When Justin went to his first high school dance, she came home from college just to be there for him.

Laura was there for us, too. She was always asking advice from Jerry, and she usually took it. She was strong and independent, but never rebellious. We always said that her greatest asset was her ability to network with other people. She would listen to others, but, in the end, we knew she would always follow her own heart. One of her friends who came to visit her in the hospital remarked, "She's the strongest woman I have ever known." Even after Laura left for college, we kept in touch by phone at least once or twice a week. Everyone wanted to talk with her, and our phone bills were enormous. She was so uplifting. That was why we needed to be there for her. For nineteen years, she had given so much joy to our family that we could spend the rest of our lives and never repay her for all that she has given to us.

Looking back, there are some things I don't want to remember; but there are also some things I don't ever want to forget. I've thought about all of the worries, things that usually never come to pass; the problems, all of the things that can be fixed; the disappointments, those things which probably could be prevented but, nevertheless, fade away in time; and tragedies, the events that change our lives forever. How much time do we spend disappointed or worried about problems over which we have so much control? How much more enjoyable would our lives be if we just took the time to appreciate what we have instead of what we want or think we need?

# IV

Six weeks after her accident, a new Laura began to emerge. She was like a butterfly carried by the winds of random events only to find herself waking up in a different time and place. At first it was frightening. Her eyes were glazed and unfocused. Her right arm moved spastically across her body. Her left side was still paralyzed. We prayed for a sign, a sign to let us know that she was fighting her way back. Then it came. On one of our daily visits to the hospital, her eyes began to focus, then follow; then finally, her arm reached out around us as we held her tightly and told her how much we loved her. It was there. It was all there: her strength, her energy, her heart, her kindness, her love for people, for life and for God. Within her badly damaged body, her spirit had not been destroyed. She just needed a way to bring it all together. She needed time, and she needed us. I prayed again that night, but this time it was a prayer of thanks. It was a prayer thanking God for saving our daughter's life.

The medical staff at Sacred Hands Rehabilitation Center held a weekly conference to evaluate her progress. There were usually ten staff members present and I was told that these conferences were scheduled to last only fifteen minutes. My daughter deserved more time than that so we always stayed much longer. Each one of the team members involved in Laura's rehabilitation would give a report. Her primary physician stated that they had begun to give her low doses of Dantrium to decrease spasticity. They would increase medication until she gained control of her right arm. She was also given bromokryptine to stimulate her mental functioning. Other than the fact that she was healing physically, he could not make any prognosis. In other words, in spite of all of his medical training, he knew very little about what was going on inside Laura's brain. He didn't know for sure if the cranial nerves running from her spinal cord through the back of her neck had been completely destroyed or were merely damaged and would eventually repair themselves. Only time would tell.

The speech pathologists had begun to work on getting Laura to swallow. They tried putting applesauce in her mouth, but she spit it out like the reflexive response of an infant. I suggested trying chocolate pudding. I knew that was one of her favorite foods. They reported that they had increased stimulation to her extremities, and, though it was slow, they were pleased with her progress. I thought about how proud I was when Laura began to read by the age of four and had made the Dean's List as a freshman in college. I thought about all the sacrifices that our family had made to put her in Montessori School, to give her private music lessons and dance lessons, and how she was the best Marie in the Nutcracker that her elementary school had ever seen. That was progress. Now I was hoping for so much more from her, just for her to be able to swallow or track an object, or maybe someday walk again.

The physical and occupational therapists worked with Laura daily. The sessions were short, only a half hour in length, and this included the time it took to take her to and from her room. During one of these sessions, they cut an orange and guided her hands as she put it to her lips. She responded by sucking. It was a response they had hoped for. Everyone in the room was silent so that Laura could concentrate entirely on this task. They repeated the task for several days, hoping for increased participation from Laura.

I sat quietly, staring in disbelief. Was this what they called experimental? Was this all that could be done for our daughter to stimulate the neurons in her brain? We could program a computer to land a spaceship on the moon, but we could think of nothing more to do for another human being than to put an orange to her lips and hope for a response. I watched the two young therapists as they wheeled Laura back to her room. They were so proud of what they had accomplished that day. I'm sure that moment has long been forgotten in their lives. But it is an image that will haunt me for the rest of my days.

We were given until the end of December for Laura to participate more actively in her therapy. If she did not, she would be dismissed from the coma stimulation program and sent to either a nursing home or a center for brain-injured patients, neither of which we found acceptable. If she did respond, she would be allowed to remain at Sacred Hands, but would be admitted into a more extensive therapy program. Either way, our insurance would not cover all of the costs. It is difficult to describe the emotional trauma that our family was experiencing with Laura's accident, only to discover that our insurance policy, into which we had paid for thirty years, would not cover all of Laura's mounting medical bills. What we thought was premier coverage turned out not to be there when we really needed it.

There were other legal matters, too. Immediately following Laura's accident, we were advised to become her legal guardians. Laura was nineteen, and for all practical purposes, an adult. If we were to make any major decisions, financial or medical, we needed guardianship and power of attorney. A court date was set.

We also needed to withdraw her from the university. We had been putting off going to her dorm room, but the semester was drawing to a close, and it was time to bring her things home.

A new student had already been assigned to take over her RA duties. We chose a day when most of the students had gone home for Christmas break. As I began to pack up her belongings that we had so lovingly carried up to her room only a few months before, I noticed a letter hanging above her desk. It was one I had written to her when she first left home. It read:

*Dear Laura,*

*This is everything you need to know before you graduate from college:*

*Work hard; do your best; don't complain or make excuses; judge others by what they do, not by the labels on their clothes; pursue excellence; pursue knowledge; listen to parents, teachers, insects, the person talking to you; sweat every day; compliment more; criticize less; hug someone when you feel you need to be hugged; brush your teeth and change your socks and underwear every day; be on time; don't let others do for you what you can do your yourself; greet people by name; don't have children until you're married; don't get married until you can afford to; set the table; keep a diary; do one thing nice every day to someone you know; do one thing nice every day to someone you don't know; read daily; exercise daily; pray daily; keep a thought in your head and a song in your heart; laugh at yourself; create solutions, not problems; and remember, always do the right thing at the right time so that you can look back on your life with few regrets.*

*Love,*
*Mom*

It was so simple. Just follow the rules and one would find happiness. I had believed that, if I just taught her to live her life with integrity, it would prepare her to face any challenge she would confront. How could I have prepared her for what she was about to face?

The days and nights of tears were beginning to wash away some of the pain. I had begun to feel numb. Depression was setting in. I was fighting it by going from one thing to another. I thought about how much of life most of us spend going from one thing to another—things, which in the long run, don't really matter. We buy things, throw away things, and shuffle things from one closet to another. We dream of things, scheme for things, go in debt for things, and occasionally sell our souls for things. All my life I had worked for things I thought were so important. And now, there wasn't a thing I wouldn't have given to have Laura back the way she was.

Friends continued to visit Laura in the hospital. It was not unusual for as many as fifteen people to be in her room at one time. It was against everything we had read about treating brain injury, but she seemed to like it. She always had the noisiest room in the dorm, so it was only fitting that she have the noisiest room in the hospital. When her friends left, our family would take a minute to read the entries they had made in her notebook. One student wrote:

*Dear Laura,*

*I knew that I was coming to visit you today. I was so happy that I sang in the shower.*

*Love,*
*Doug*

21

We knew this enthusiasm would help Laura recover. However, in spite of the fact that Laura appeared to enjoy these visits, she was becoming exhausted. At one of the staff meetings, all of the therapists reported that she was too tired to participate in her therapy sessions. She was not getting enough down time and visitation would have to be limited. I took advantage of the quiet times which followed. Sometimes I read to her. Sometimes I rubbed her feet. Sometimes I just held her and prayed. During one visit, I picked up a Bible. It was a large print version and the only thing I could read through my tears. Inside was a list of verses on healing. The Bible had been left by a family whose children Laura had cared for the summer before. They had told us how calm she had always seemed before her accident, and they marveled at how well she was able to manage their children. They loved her and wanted her back, too. They explained to us their religious beliefs and asked if they could pray for her. They knew that God was going to heal her.

Their religious beliefs didn't seem to matter at that point. They were seeking the same spiritual healing that we were all seeking: a power from within, yet beyond human conception; a power greater than the sum of all earthly parts. How we define that power is insignificant, and how we intellectualize the paths on which we seek that power seems even less significant. I began to wonder if religion indeed wasn't merely an individual's attempt to create order out of a randomly disordered universe. Were we using religion to make sense out of Laura's accident, or did God really have a plan for our lives?

I told Jaime once that someday something good would come from all of this. He said, "I didn't need this to make me a better person. I just didn't need this at all."

When I discussed this conversation with a close friend, he said, "Yes, but many people do." Was that why God had chosen someone so young, so beautiful, so innocent to teach us what we already knew, but had forgotten in the busyness of our daily lives? Laura connected with everyone with whom she came into contact. Perhaps that was the reason for which we were searching.

Laura was so different during our quiet times together. She was never agitated and didn't thrash about as she often did with other people in the room. She lay in her bed or sat very still in her wheelchair. At times she appeared to be asleep. But when I stopped to look at her, one eye would open, and she would focus intently on my face. I didn't know if she fully recognized me or not. I thought of how a baby always knew when it was being held by its mother. I knew, too, that my presence had stirred in her a love stronger than anything else in the world and a memory of other times, long ago, when I had held her and read to her and told her of things to come.

Each day Laura made small steps toward recovery. But each day, the daughter we had reared was slipping further and further away. She was beginning to take on many of the characteristics of people we had seen in institutions. Her hair, which had been partially shaved prior to surgery, was beginning to grow out at different lengths, and it was difficult to keep clean. Her face lacked expression, and she was functioning on the level of a three-month-old in an adult body, with memories somewhere in between.

She was always on my mind, day and night, and I'd often lie awake for hours wondering, hoping, and praying. The emotional strain was taking a physical toll on my body, and I developed walking pneumonia. I couldn't see Laura for several days. I found myself instead wandering aimlessly through stores, seeing things that I wanted to buy for her. We had often talked about what kind of home she would have, where she would register for her wedding, and now she seemed to be everywhere I went. How I ended up at a bookstore perusing the section on grief, I do not know. I was looking for something on *how to*, a magic self-help book that would get us through this. I paged through everything, but everything seemed so superfluous. What I discovered is that there is no such formula. Grief has no rules. There is no set amount of time that it will take to recover. The experience is deeply personal and many will never get over what they have lost. It's as if one's world were suddenly turned upside down and nothing ever realigns the same. Everything appears distorted and out of place. Relationships are redefined, routines are reestablished, and interests are replaced with new priorities. In short, what I was experiencing was the same inner metaphysical metamorphosis that had manifested itself in the outward appearance of my daughter.

That weekend, my husband gave up two tickets to a Packers game at Lambeau Field. He was changing, too.

Grief is a natural and necessary reaction to loss. It is a process of gradually letting go of what was and what might have been. There comes a point, however, when it no longer fulfills its purpose but becomes destructive instead. I had reached that point. It was time to look up and not down, out and not in. If I was going to help Laura, I needed to become a whole person again.

Once I asked a friend who had experienced a similar loss how long it would take for the pain to go away, and she said, "A very long time." I asked her to pray for us because she seemed to have a direct line to God. Her response was, "You have a direct line, too. You just need to pull on it a little harder."

There will come a time when Laura, too, will grieve—when she realizes what she has lost, what she might have become, and must accept whatever challenges are set before her. The Lord's Prayer will have new meaning for her life, as well as for ours. It is no longer *my* will be done. It is *thy* will be done.

Life itself is such a precious gift, and we take it so for granted. Yet the inequities of it are so difficult to understand. How could it be that someone with so much potential becomes so limited, while others limit themselves and live well beyond their allotted years? Life isn't fair. It isn't just. It just is.

# V

Laura met Hanns when she was sixteen. She was interested in another boy at the time. When Hanns learned that she was going to a school dance with someone else, he did what any other love-smitten teenager would do. He toilet papered the front of our house. My husband was irate. He phoned Hanns' mother and told her that if Hanns was not over within an hour to clean up the mess, he was going to call the police. Hanns was there. His mother warned him never to get too close to Laura for fear of what her father might do.

It wasn't long before they fell in love and Hanns started calling me Mom. There was no doubt in his mind that he was going to be part of our family someday. Their relationship was refreshing. There wasn't a week that went by when Hanns didn't do something crazy for her. One day there were a dozen long stemmed red roses on her desk at school. Another day there would be a package of treats with a love note by our back door. They'd talk for hours on the phone, sometimes long distance, much to her father's annoyance. But they had so much fun and were so good to each other.

When Laura needed a ride, Hanns was there. When Laura had her wisdom teeth pulled, Hanns was there. When Laura had her accident, Hanns was there again. He heard about it at two in the morning and rushed to the hospital to be with her. When he arrived, he fell into my arms and sobbed.

I don't know how long Hanns will continue to be at her side. There will come a time when he will have to make a choice. Parents do not have that choice. For now, he continues to visit, and with the rest of us he hopes and prays that she will recover. After one of his visits, Hanns left the following note:

*Dear Laura,*

*Today is the best day I have had in two months. Laura, you grabbed my hand and kissed it when I came in. I almost started to cry. You mean so much to me. I can't imagine life w/out you. I love you, sweetheart. You are my inspiration to live.*

*Love always and forever,*
*Hanns*

Jenna was also there for Laura. They were like sisters. When Laura was four, Jenna's parents had placed an ad in our local paper seeking day care. I answered the ad and it seemed a perfect match. Both Laura and Jenna would attend morning kindergarten, ride the bus home together from school, then be playmates for the remainder of the afternoon. Jenna visited Laura in the hospital every chance she could, and when she couldn't, she wrote letters. This is one of them.

*Dear Laura,*

*Where do I begin? It's going to be hard going through the holidays without you. It just seems like it's been so long without you. I want you back. I need you back. It's been fifteen wonderful years. We have so many great memories with each other. I miss calling you on the phone and hearing about your dates with Hanns. I miss being able to road map it to the mall or whatnot. And I miss complaining about things that I know you'd understand. You really take the little things for granted and then when something like this happens, it's the little things that you miss more than anything. You will always have a special place in my heart. You will always be my best friend. I love ya, La.*

*Always and forever,*
*Jenna*

There were other friends, too. Laura had met Sally during her freshman year at Whitewater. They shared everything. Sally was at the hospital as soon as she heard the news of Laura's accident, and she continued to be at Laura's bedside during the months that followed. She wrote letters, too.

*Dear Laura,*

*Every so often someone comes along who makes you want to become everything you can possibly want to become. You have been that person to me. I love you, Laura, always.*

*Sally*

Other letters were left in the journal by friends we had never met. One letter seemed to summarize so much:

*Hi Laura,*

*I came to see you with Hanns today. You've made such marked improvement over the last week. You look great. It's obvious your body and spirit have been working hard. You keep it up! You are the most affectionate patient I have ever seen. You had tons of kisses from Hanns, just couldn't get enough. It was great to hold your hand. It was so warm. You're napping now. Keep refueling. You're making incredible progress. We can all see it. The love around you from your family and friends is immense, which is really no surprise cuz you are so loved and such a tremendous person. Keep up the hard work. Will see you with that contagious smile again soon.*

*Much love,*
*Bo*

I thought they would be there for the long haul.

# VI

Tragedy is a testimony to the human spirit to survive. It is also a testimony to triumph. Eight weeks after her accident, Jerry and I were sitting by Laura's bed at Sacred Hands. Her eyes were closed, her face expressionless, her left arm clenched tightly to her side, her body silent and still. Suddenly, the fingers on her right hand began to move. I recognized the positions. She was forming the letters of the alphabet in sign language. We were ecstatic. For the first time since her accident, Laura showed recognizable signs of cognitive functioning. She could think!

The next day, Laura said, "I love you" in sign.

Laura continued to make slow, steady progress. She began to communicate more and more through her fingers. We learned that the psychologist who had been working with Laura was fluent in sign, and we hoped that he would help her reconnect with the world around her. She told him with her fingers that she knew the year and the month and where she was. She told us things, too, but we were not quick enough to pick up on them.

The day after Christmas we received a letter from someone we had never met. He had read about Laura's accident in the newspaper on Washington Island, and he wanted us to know that he had been praying for her. He also quoted a passage from scripture: "Nothing is impossible with God." The verse echoed through my mind as we drove toward the hospital. That evening, strange things began to happen. First, streetlights flickered, then they went dark as we passed under them. It could have been a coincidence, but, then again, maybe it wasn't. When Jerry and I looked at each other, we were thinking the same thing. We each had felt a presence, a sort of cosmic energy, a power greater than ourselves.

When we arrived at the hospital, Laura was lying quietly in bed, staring blankly into space. We talked for a while, then put her in her wheelchair and took her down the elevator into the chapel. There was a small Christmas tree in one corner of the chapel and a crèche with the baby Jesus in another. Justin played some of his old favorites on the piano while we talked. Laura was beginning to get restless so we decided to leave, but the door leading back into the hospital had locked behind us. Laura became more restless and struggled to get out of her wheelchair. We realized that she wanted to walk. We all looked at each other and said, "Why not?" Jerry held one arm, Jaime the other. I held her waist from behind and Justin guided her feet. And there, at Christmas, in front of the baby Jesus, in a quiet little chapel on a cold December night, Laura took her first steps. She was not only surrounded by the love of her family, she was supported by that strange cosmic force that we had felt on the way to the hospital. Some call it the Holy Spirit.

When we were ready to leave the chapel, the door leading to the hospital had mysteriously reopened. We walked quietly back to the room. Laura gave us the sign for chapel, and with her fingers told us that she wanted to walk again. We told her that we would be back the next day. If she was determined, so were we.

The following day, we received a two-page letter from the medical staff chastising us for what we had done.

Driving home from the hospital that night, I thought back to the time when Laura had learned sign language. She was in the fourth grade. Her teacher had just lost a son in a similar car accident, on a similar night, on a similar dark road. She was teaching sign language for him, to carry on his spirit. It all began to fit, like a piece to a giant puzzle, as if it were part of a plan we were not meant to understand. Was there a connection between the son's death and Laura's survival, some sort of mystical energy flow of which we had become an integral part?

I thought back, too, to the night of Laura's accident and the route her body had taken. From the first call to 911 and the arrival of the fireman who cut her out of the tangled metal, to the ambulance driver who helped her into the helicopter, to the trauma physician on duty at Froedtert, to the neurosurgeons in intensive care, to the social workers, the speech and physical therapists, the nursing staff, etc., etc. It was like she had been placed on a medical conveyor belt. Each person treated only the physical symptoms with which they were confronted. When they had accomplished their goals, as they saw fit, they passed her on to the next professional in line, never seeing much beyond those who came immediately before or after. No one but us ever saw Laura as a whole person from beginning to end.

New Year's Eve came and went, and, like Christmas, it was not one we wish to remember. For the past thirty years, we have gotten together with another family. We have watched their children grow up and they have watched ours. We missed getting together only twice: one time because of a blizzard; another, chicken pox. It is not easy to find marriages that grow closer with time, much less friendships. We have been fortunate to find both. When we got together, rather than making resolutions— which are never kept—we made predictions. We have developed a rather elaborate system for doing this, making predictions in categories ranging from sports to politics to family to personal, etc. One person volunteers to record the predictions. They are then sealed in an envelope until the following year when they're read to the group. The one with the most correct predictions scores points, although nothing is ever done with them. Then new predictions are made. The game has always generated lively discussions. This year we did not play the game. No one wanted to read last year's predictions. No one could have predicted what had happened. No one had any idea what next year could possibly bring. No one, that is, except Justin. At fourteen, his innocence made him the most resilient, yet also the most vulnerable, to all that had taken place in our lives.

# VII

For some unknown reason, the bones of people with brain injury heal much faster than those of normal people. The fractures in Laura's hips had completely healed, as had her arm, which had been surgically repaired with a metal plate. The physical therapists were given the go ahead to let Laura's legs bear more weight. They followed a procedure for transferring her body from the bed to the wheelchair and insisted that we follow the exact procedure. Once each day, Laura was given range of motion exercises to stimulate circulation in her limbs. This was to keep her muscles from becoming rigid, as was happening on Laura's left side.

During the first week of January, Laura returned to Froedtert Hospital for a comparative CAT scan and consultation with her physician. It was seventeen degrees below zero that morning. We bundled Laura up, and I rode with her in a medical van to the hospital. Jerry met us there. As we sat in the examination room, a woman wearing a white medical jacket entered. She looked at Laura, then at us. Then she asked, "Do you remember me?"

Jerry and I both answered, "Yes." It was Nurse Death carrying her shingle. She studied the x-rays, then Laura.

Finally, she said, "That Laura is doing as well as she is, is nothing short of a miracle." We knew. We all knew.

Within weeks, Laura moved from infancy to toddlerhood. She was showing some facial expressions and mouthing *I love you* and *home*. One night, I received a call from Hanns. He had been with her at the hospital, and he wanted to let me know that she was calling out "Mom." She did have a voice! It was the first time since her accident that it was heard. More words would come, and the proposed laser surgery on her vocal chords would probably not be necessary.

She was moving around more in bed, her right side thrashing uncontrollably, and the staff felt she had to be restrained for her own safety. She was tied to the bed. Finally, she was put in something called a vale bed, which we called the blue cage. It gave her room to move around and us some relief.

The speech therapists were feeding Laura pureed foods in an attempt to teach her to swallow. Who would have ever thought that was a skill that had to be learned, or, in Laura's case, relearned? But if food did not go down the esophagus and instead went down the trachea, it would accumulate in the lungs and possibly lead to pneumonia. They considered putting a radioactive dye in the food and taking x-rays as it went down Laura's throat. They would not try liquids until they were certain that the pureed food was entering the correct channel.

Now that Laura could stand with assistance, she was placed periodically on the commode. I remember when Laura first used her potty chair. We bought her training pants with lace and pink bows on the back. She was so cute and we were so proud. However, there is nothing cute about an adult child relearning to control bodily functions.

In January, Laura was dismissed from the coma stimulation program and entered the acute rehabilitation program at Sacred Hands. Her therapy increased to three hours per day. She was beginning to stay awake for longer periods of time, but she had difficulty concentrating on any one thing. She began to say "home" constantly and there were times when she refused to work with the therapists. They often relied on us to get her to respond to commands, because she would do what we asked. We brought in photo albums, flash cards, calendars, alphabet signs, anything to get her to respond. She had very little control over her arms but she was able to signal *yes* or *no* with a nod of her head when asked questions. Although she could read a few words, her speech was slow and monotone. We hoped in time that she would become more coherent.

One night, on one of my usual visits to the hospital, I found Laura lying in bed, a Mozart CD playing in the background. We had asked the nursing staff to play classical music, particularly Mozart, during her quiet times. We had read that it helped to increase IQ scores, and we hoped that it would help her brain cells reconnect. Her feeding tube had leaked all over her bed and she was soaking wet. She was feeling her hair and noticed for the first time that it had been cut short. I called for a nurse, and we changed her clothes and put her into her wheelchair. I took her into the bathroom and wheeled her by the sink to wash her face. "You're beautiful," I told her. She looked into the mirror.

"No more," she responded. I put my arms around her. It was a bittersweet moment. Laura was becoming aware of what had happened to her, but she could no longer reach out or cry.

When Laura had been a little girl, I would say to her, "The first thing you put on when you get dressed in the morning is a smile."

Now, I watched as Laura put a smile back on her face. "You're beautiful," she said, then turned and asked why I was crying. I would tell her the story some day, but not now.

My daughter was coming back to me, little by little.

# VIII

The brain is an incredible organ. It weighs three pounds and is the approximate size of two fists. It contains over one hundred billion neurons, more than stars in the Milky Way. Each day, the average brain will lose as many as fifty thousand neurons. They can never be replaced. As we age, our brain shrinks in size due, in part, to lost neurons.

The brain peaks in development between the ages eighteen and twenty-five. However, the average sixty year old's brain contains four times the information as the average twenty year old's and three times the vocabulary. The brain of a younger person is just much quicker at responding to stimuli.

Attached to the neurons are axons and dendrites. Axons carry messages from the neurons, dendrites carry messages to the neurons. Between the neurons are gaps called synapses. These synapses are about a millionth of an inch in width. Messages cross these synapses by means of neurotransmitters.

At the base of the brain is the brain stem. This is what attaches the brain to the spinal cord. Above the brain stem is the cerebellum, which regulates balance and coordination. Next to that is the thalamus, which organizes our senses. Also located near the brain stem is the hippocampus, which converts short-term memory to long term memory, and the hypothalamus, which regulates the nervous system and controls emotions. Surrounding these areas is the cerebral cortex. It is where most thinking takes place and where much of our information is stored.

When a person's brain is injured, it usually swells and begins to put pressure on the brain stem and all of the areas surrounding it. If the brain swells into the brain stem, it can shut off the area of the nervous system which controls the heart and lungs. This is the reason why people die from brain injury, which is the number one cause of death to people between the ages of one and forty-four. To avoid this, a tube is often inserted into the brain to drain spinal fluid and allow some space for swelling. This is a relatively new procedure, and, in recent years, it has saved many lives, including our daughter's.

If the impact to the brain is severe, the brain can be torn from the brain stem. This is called shearing. The space between neurons increases and messages do not get transmitted. This is why people with brain injury have difficulty with speech, coordination, and short-term memory. Since the nerves leading from the brain to the spinal cord cross at the neck, one side of the body often becomes partially paralyzed, a condition referred to as hemi-paralysis. Most people with brain injury will have a weakness on one side of their body. One eye might be enlarged or the person might have difficulty focusing; one arm might be clenched, or the person might walk with a slight to noticeable limp. Sometimes the brain will sustain additional and more serious injury as it bounces against the inside of the skull. This is what happened to Laura. The left side of her body became paralyzed while the right side of her body suffered uncontrollable ataxia.

When brain tissue dies, it turns into a fluid that can put pressure on other brain tissue. Occasionally, this fluid is reabsorbed into the body through the spinal cord. If this does not occur, it must be drained surgically. A CAT scan three months after Laura's accident showed signs of brain fluid. Another CAT scan was scheduled for the following month and would reveal whether or not it had been absorbed by her body. In the meantime, she would be watched for signs of regression: an increased need for sleep and an increased difficulty with balance. Her injury could not have been much worse.

Most of what is known about the brain has only been discovered within the past twenty-five years. CAT scans can reveal areas of the brain which have sustained damage, and physicians can label those areas and perform surgical techniques to keep a person alive, but beyond that, very little is known about how a person will function after the brain has been injured. No one can predict what deficits a person will have. There is no pattern to follow. No two injuries are alike. No two brains are identical.

The brain functions like an intricate game of Scrabble. Every word, every thought, every behavior builds upon itself. As new information is gathered and new insights are formed, the gaps between the words are filled in. Experience is what holds all the letters in place. When brain injury occurs, it's as if someone threw a handful of pieces into the air. Ideas are jumbled and words are left dangling in mid thought. Some pieces are missing altogether and can never be replaced. It will take time to put it all back together again.

Somewhere hidden deep within the brain is the *mind*. It is the basis upon which all else is built. Like the first word in Scrabble, it covers the star—one's inner being, one's soul. *Mind* is an acronym for who we are. *M* is for morality: the sense of right and wrong. *I* is for imagination: the ability to form images of that which we cannot see. *N* is for need: the need to survive, surpass, and surmount the obstacles, which have been placed in our way. And *D* is for determination: the commitment to purpose, the strength of our convictions, the energy with which we face life. The mind is the only part of our bodies that cannot be touched by medical science.

Although Laura's brain was injured and the words and ideas in her brain were scrambled, her mind was intact. Her inner core, her sense of self, her love for God, for people, for life was not damaged. All learning takes place by association, and we became the link between her mind and reality. Laura would rebuild. The pathways in her brain would reroute. Neurons would find new ways to connect. And we would be there to help, every step of the way.

The mind forms at conception. It grows with every touch of love, when we are nurtured as infants and encouraged by those with whom we come into contact as we grow into adulthood. I've often wondered why some people just don't get it; why some people, particularly children, refuse to learn; why some information can be taught, only to be forgotten the following day. It all goes back to the M-I-N-D, to our childhood, to the day we were born.

I have seen many children who have never developed a sense of right and wrong. They were punished for good behavior or rewarded for bad. They never learned to trust anyone—their family, their teachers, their peers, even themselves. I have seen children who have been ignored and who have been placed in front of the television set for hours on end, or have been left unattended in their cribs, only to cry themselves to sleep. They were seldom read to or encouraged to engage in creative play; and, as a result, they never developed a sense of wonder or envisioned a future that would demand excellence on their part. I have seen children showered with material possessions, but lacking purpose. They have never developed the need to achieve. They have become satisfied with mediocrity, too young and too early. I have seen children who perceive strength in physical rather than spiritual terms. They lack character and commitment. All that we are capable of being begins with our moral values, our imaginations, our needs, and our determination—the *MIND*. It is who we are and is reflected in all that we do.

# IX

A Moment in Time
frozen
still

Memory,
like slides across a screen
fading with age
yet timeless

So Many Moments,
all in a jar
a picture
a teddy bear

They are You
They are Me
They are what connect us
and make us one
but not whole
not complete
not alive.

I felt as if I were wandering around inside a large cardboard box. It was dark inside. Images of Laura from the time she was born would flash out of sequence across the walls of the box. Juxtaposed were images of her since the accident—at Froedtert in intensive care, at Sacred Hands in her wheelchair, driving down the road on the night of the accident in her new red car. Sometimes I would hear her calling me, "Mom, don't leave." Sometimes I'd hear her telling me about what she was doing at school. Sometimes I'd hear her scream as her car slammed against the tree. Sometimes I'd be driving her car wishing that I could have been there in her place.

The voices would sometimes begin quietly, with a phone call or a baby crying or seeing the picture of a young girl in a magazine. They would crescendo until all of the sounds blended into one, then echo from side to side, never in tune with the images. Tears would begin to fill the box. The images would disappear, and it would be quiet again—for a moment.

On the outside of the box were pictures of Laura in the future. On one wall, Laura would be sitting in a wheelchair, her left side still paralyzed, her right side moving uncontrollably. She is in a nursing home. I can see doctors and nurses holding onto their charts and staring at that picture, all nodding their heads in agreement. There was another picture on the other side of the box. It was where most of our friends stood. It showed Laura having made a complete comeback. She is just finishing college, getting ready to be married, and planning a future with children. Finally, there was a picture of Laura on the very top of the box. No one could reach it. Only God could see it. It was covered by a calendar that seemed to go on for eternity. On the cover of the calendar was written *Have Faith*.

Sleeping pills got me through the nights. Determination to get Laura back on the road to recovery got me through the days.

# X

Laura began to ask for Hanns. He came on weekends. He couldn't stay, and yet he couldn't stay away. They would hug and kiss and wink at each other. Laura's eyes would light up when she saw him. I couldn't read Hanns' eyes. His mother visited the hospital to see how Laura was doing. She told me that she had hoped that someday Laura would have been her daughter-in-law. I told her that I still had that hope. She didn't respond. She brought a bouquet of beautiful flowers with a note that read:

*Dear Laura,*

*You have always been the sweetest person in the whole world. You still are.*

*Love,*
*Monika*

I finally wrote to Hanns.

*Dear Hanns,*

*It has been fourteen weeks since Laura's accident—fourteen weeks, two days and fifteen hours, to be exact. There isn't a minute of the day or night that I don't think about her. This has devastated our lives, and I can only imagine what it has done to yours. Laura loves you very much. She asks about you all the time. I know you love her, too. You can't love someone for three years and then suddenly just stop loving them. I know, too, that you talked about getting married someday. It will be a long time before you can talk about that again. If you never do, I'll understand. You don't need to decide that today. All I know is that right now you are a very important part of her recovery. She needs you now as a friend. You two spent so much time together these past three years and have so many experiences for her to connect with—experiences that we don't have. I know she'll recover. I'm not expecting the moon, just a miracle.*

*I know how important it is for you to go on with your life and I won't ever get in your way or ask you to do anything you don't want to do. I'm just asking for all the help you can give because I love her so. I love you too, Hanns.*

*Love,*
*"Mom"*

At the end of January, we returned to Froedtert Hospital for another CAT scan. The fluid on the top of Laura's brain had disappeared. It had been reabsorbed into her body. There was nothing more surgically that could be done to improve her condition. She had reached the limits of medical science. It was wait and watch. Which cranial nerves would reconnect? Which would not? There were twelve.

The first nerve has to do with smell and taste. Laura had had very little interest in food up to this point. She was still being fed through a tube in her stomach. Since she did not eat normally, a fungus developed in her mouth and throat. She was given medication to counteract it, but her mouth still needed to be cleaned several times a day.

The second cranial nerve affects vision. Laura appeared to be able to see a little, although we were not certain what she was seeing or if she was interpreting what she was seeing correctly. She recognized family members but continued to call a rectangle a square.

The third, fourth, and sixth cranial nerves work together to control eye movement, pupil response, and the ability to open the eyelids. These nerves are also responsible for allowing the eyes to move in sync. Laura's left eye did not open for several months. The pupil was blown and did not respond to light. It had changed color, to a slightly different blue, and was dilated and wouldn't contract. It was like a camera with a broken shutter. She would most likely be affected by this the rest of her life.

The fifth cranial nerve affects facial sensation and the muscular movements involved in chewing. The seventh nerve affects facial movement, raising the eyebrows, and smiling. This Laura would need to relearn. We spent hours having her imitate our facial expressions. Justin was great at this.

The eighth cranial nerve, like the second, is a more specialized nerve. It is responsible for hearing and for balance. It is the nerve that tells the brain where the body is in time and space. At one point in the brain stem, the nerves that control hearing and balance join together; at another point, they separate. That is why a person who is hearing impaired can usually walk, whereas a person with brain injury might not be able to hear or walk. Laura appeared to have difficulty with both. She complained that she could not hear. The medical staff at Sacred Hands treated her hearing loss with medication, suggesting that it might be due to wax buildup. There did not seem to be any improvement. The psychologist thought it might be due to Laura's inability to process verbal communication. The neurologist suggested that it might be due to a dysfunction of the eighth cranial nerve causing Laura not to be able to respond to auditory stimuli. He asked Laura if she could hear herself talk, and she said, "No." The eighth cranial nerve is one of the least forgiving when the brain has been injured. If it was responsible for Laura's hearing loss, it could be permanent. An appointment with a hearing specialist was made to rule out other causes.

The ninth cranial nerve involves the body's ability to protect airways and to open the vocal chords. It also controls the gag reflex. It prevents food and fluid from going down the trachea and causing a person to choke. This is why people who have been brain injured cannot immediately resume normal eating patterns. They must be introduced to food slowly, beginning first with solids that can be easily swallowed, such as yogurt, pudding, tapioca, etc. Liquids, such as water, require a mental response that is too quick. They slide into the trachea where they accumulate, and possibly lead to infection, including pneumonia. Chewing is a whole other skill that was yet to come.

The tenth cranial nerve controls the heart rate and blood pressure. When this nerve is damaged, a person often experiences something called neurostorming. The blood pressure rises out of control and the body perspires profusely. The arms will usually posture inward. Death can result if this is not controlled with medication. Laura experienced neurostorming for quite some time after her accident. It was the most frightening thing I have ever seen.

The eleventh cranial nerve affects movement in the neck. I remember the day that Laura first showed signs of being able to hold her head up. We were ecstatic, although it would be a long time before she could go without a headrest on her wheelchair.

The twelfth cranial nerve controls tongue movement. When people have been brain injured, they have difficulty using their tongues to eat or to speak. Letters such as k, g, s, t, etc., require considerable muscular control. Brain injured people not only have difficulty speaking, they have difficulty being understood. I can't imagine the frustration that Laura will encounter if she is unable to communicate with the world around her. If only these nerves could be reconnected surgically! A magic electrode could fuse it all together. For Laura, it was like repairing the main wiring of her brain in the dark. The psychologist indicated that Laura was already beginning to show signs of frustration at her limitations. That awareness was, tragically, a good sign.

The bones in Laura's arm had healed but the limb showed little movement. If her brain did not tell her muscles to move, they would atrophy. The bones would begin to lose mineral density. Future fractures could occur. Laura received both active and passive therapy on her arm. Her friend Sally would come to the hospital to do her nails. It helped Laura move her fingers and hands. I don't think Sally realized how important her therapy was in helping Laura to recover.

That same week we learned that an investigation of the accident revealed that Laura had nothing to do with the cause of it. This was supposed to be good news. If only it would bring my daughter back.

For months I lived somewhere in that place between *sleep* and *awake*. I began to withdraw more and more—from stores that showed beautiful models wearing clothes that would have appeared stunning on Laura; and from people, who would say things like, "Well, maybe she won't ever be normal," or "She could spend the rest of her life in an institution, you know."

Some people would tell me stories about people with brain injuries who would get stuck asking what time it was. They thought it was funny and would make me laugh. I knew it was damage to the frontal lobe of the brain, which caused most brain-injured victims to get stuck on words, and I didn't think that was very funny. I was too vulnerable. Every day I would climb a mountain of hope only to fall again into the valley of doubt and despair. Laura was but a shadow of her former self, and it followed me everywhere.

Piles began to accumulate around the house—ironing that hadn't been done in months, lessons that I had planned teach, books that I had hoped to read. At the bottom of one of these piles was a list made out on October 23, the day of Laura's accident. It went on for pages—things I had planned to do, to purchase, to accomplish. I threw the list away, along with other things that had piled on top of it. There would be new lists: things for Laura—rehab plans, laundry from the hospital, and ways to help Jerry and Jaime and Justin to cope and get on with their lives. I didn't have the strength to make that list just yet.

A friend from church called. I told her that I just couldn't go on anymore. She said, "You will. You will find the strength, and you will rise to the occasion." It was easy for her to say. It would be a long time before I understood what she meant.

I had returned to teaching shortly after Laura's accident. I had difficulty staying focused and relied heavily on years of experience. One day, a colleague entered my room and said, "You're lucky."

"Right," I told him. "I'll be lucky when I have my daughter back."

"You're still lucky," he repeated and left the room.

I didn't know why he would say that. He knew what had happened. Was it because Laura was still alive? Was it because I still had a wonderful husband and family, a beautiful home, a good job, and my health? The more I tried to figure out how

I could possibly be lucky at a time like this, the more reasons I came up with for being so.

That night I saw more progress in Laura. Maybe it was because I was looking for it. I also saw things that I hadn't noticed before. A new patient had arrived at the hospital. He was Laura's age and a track star. He had been in a car accident, too. He had been adjusting the radio when his car went out of control, flipped over, and burst into flames. His body was badly burned and part of his skull had been removed. He was barely conscious. There were other patients as well—a young boy who had fallen out of a silo, a teenager with a broken neck and broken jaw in addition to his brain injury, an elderly woman who had fallen down her basement stairs and was still in a coma—all on one floor, in one hospital, in one city, hidden behind our morning newspapers, our catalogs, our traffic jams, our long lines at the supermarket, and all of the billboards of our daily lives. Some had families who sat tirelessly at their bedsides or wheeled them up and down the hospital corridors, exhaustion and despair written all over their faces. Others had no one at all.

"You're very lucky," a nurse said to Laura as she entered the room. This time I knew why. Her left arm clenched tightly to her body, her head and right arm shook from ataxia, and her eyes showed no understanding of where she was or what had happened to her. But she had her life and she had us. I had learned more that day than in all the years spent at the universities. They were things that could not be taught from a textbook. All the way home, I kept saying to myself: *Don't dwell on the past, thank God for today, look forward to tomorrow.* If Laura could smile, I would try to smile, too.

# XI

Life is all about awareness—making connections within ourselves, to our surroundings, to the past, the present and the future; and between that which we can see, hear, touch and smell and that which we cannot. We tried everything to help Laura make those connections. We showed her flash cards, photo albums, small keyboards, Mozart, recordings of songs she played on the piano, only to discover that much of what we did, she could not hear and did not process. She could not remember the accident or any of the events during the months that had led up to it.

When a person's brain has been injured, much of the information in the short-term memory is lost, and it is difficult to put new information into the long-term memory without access to the short-term memory. Perhaps this is God's way of helping Laura deal with the tragic events of her life. People often learn to compensate by carrying a notebook to remind them of what they had done or what they must do. For Laura this will be difficult unless she regains control of her arms.

I have often heard educators refer to learning as *drill and kill*. They are so afraid of repetition for fear students might become bored with learning. As I watch Laura attempt to put the events of her life back in order, I have come to realize how important repetition is. It takes a long time for information to become part of one's long-term memory, months of repetition for it to become incorporated into one's patterns of thinking. Our schools have become entertainment centers, and knowledge is more like sensory stimuli disconnected from the relevance of an individual's past or future. We teach too much in the present. We learn too much from the past. Perhaps *drill and kill* should be changed to *drill and instill*. Memory is a record of all of the events of our past, and those memories are the building blocks upon which all future experiences are based. Repetition is the mortar that binds it all together.

When a person has been brain injured, he becomes unaware of himself. Hygiene, clothing, personal habits are not important, because they do not exist in the mind of the brain injured. As Laura recovers, her sense of self will begin to return. I do not know, however, to what extent. On every visit to the hospital, I followed a routine of washing her face and brushing her teeth. On one visit, she told me, "Not while people are here." She was beginning to show signs of awareness.

Our sense of awareness expands outward from inside the self, connecting first with our families and those we love. This is why it is so important for parents to spend time with their children, especially when they are young. It is during the first few months of life that children develop an awareness of the type of world they will enter. Will it be loving or hostile, caring or contemptuous? Will they be able to rely on people they love, or must they go it alone? Will others turn away when they cry, or will they learn to trust, to network, and to move beyond their own needs to help others? In our world of daycare centers and "get the most out of life" mentality, we have lost sight of so many of the things that are truly important.

# XII

Tears warmed my pillow. Dusk faded into dawn; dawn into dusk. I no longer saw color. People passed by without faces. My heart was broken into pieces too small to ever put back together again. *Help me, God. Please help me. I cannot go on. Bring my daughter back. Help her to recover her life ...*

Jerry called from the hospital. The chaplain had just arrived. He told Jerry that, when the burden gets too heavy to carry, he should call on the Big Guy above. I said, "I did. I prayed all the way home, and he didn't listen."

"He must have," Jerry responded. "She's better tonight."

I was angry—angry at people telling me what I had to accept, angry at the suggestion that medication would change what had happened, angry at students who could learn but wouldn't, angry that I had spent my whole life working hard and trying to do the right thing, and angry that I didn't cause this accident to happen. Anger is a great motivator. I was fighting my way back, too.

On the first Saturday in February, we toured Lakeside Rehabilitation Center in southeast Wisconsin. On the way home, we passed the spot where Laura had her accident. We could still see the red paint where her car had struck the tree.

That night I had a dream, a dream that someone dressed in soft black leather from head to toe was standing by my bed. He slipped his hands into my chest cavity and pulled out my beating heart. Then he smashed it against the tree where it splattered, coagulating in drips until it covered all of the red paint. The man in leather then slithered out of the room as quietly as he had entered. I woke up in a sweat.

The alarm had rung and it was time to get ready for church. I could not feel my heartbeat. I checked for scars on my chest. There were none. But my heart was gone.

As I sat in church and closed my eyes to pray, the image of the paint and the tree and the man in black leather stayed with me. Suddenly, the color of the paint on the tree began to change to a deeper, richer red. In the distance of my mind I heard a whisper. At first I could not understand. "This is the blood of Christ." It grew louder. "This is the blood of Christ," and louder, until finally I felt a tug at my arm. It was Jerry holding the communion plate. The minister was holding a cup in front of the congregation. "This is the blood of Christ," he said. "It was shed for you." I drank. The organist played: *This is the bread of life.* For the first time in four months, I felt peace.

We drove from church to the hospital to pick up Laura. We were taking her home for a visit. She had not been home since shortly before her accident. Jaime met us at the hospital. He had taken off work the Friday before to be trained by the physical therapists in transferring her into and out of her wheelchair. All the way home, we pointed out places that would help spark her memory—her old high school, the shopping center where we would go to on Sundays during football season, the clothing store where she had once worked, and all of the houses in our neighborhood. It was a wonderful day. I made her some of her favorite foods, and, for a time, we sat on the couch together, like we had done so many times before. But most of the afternoon was spent in her room, lying on her bed and writing to her. She still could not hear.

We told her many things—about the car, the accident, and what had happened to her. She told us that her favorite part of being home was her family and that she didn't want to go back to the hospital. She told us that she did not like the way she was. She had talked about going home for so long; and somehow, I think in her mind she thought that everything would be the way it was when she returned, but it wasn't. We knew better.

Laura's brain was potholed with memory lapses. She could remember being a student at Whitewater. She could remember the classes she took as a freshman. But she couldn't remember the fall or being an RA or the many new friends she had made and the wonderful experiences they had together. Parts of her life were gone. We would have to tell her about them. There would be new experiences, although from here on, she would have difficulty remembering them.

Hanns arrived for dinner. He sat next to Laura and fed her tiny bits of lasagna. His love was very deep and very blind. He wrote notes to her, and they hugged and kissed goodbye. Hanns returned to Whitewater; Laura, to the hospital.

# XIII

Patience ... patience ... patience! Want to make God laugh? Try planning. We were learning to live our lives one day at a time.

Throughout our journey in this world, we are continually seeking—guidance from our parents, advice from our friends, inspiration from those who have found a deeper meaning in the mysteries of life. We move beyond the fables of Aesop as a child and into the philosophical realm of those who walked this earth before us: Plato and Socrates, who sought truth and order through reason; Cicero, who reduced words to emotionless rhetoric; and Shakespeare, who used words to play with our emotions. They were of this world, their human inspirations limited only by that which could not be accepted on faith.

But the universe is more complicated than that. Our lives are more like fragments of a giant mirror drifting in myriad dimensions throughout the cosmos. Unless we seek insight through divine inspiration, our journeys on this earth will be aimless, and we will see only reflections of ourselves in that which we hold so close. Our search for answers all comes down to only one question—why?

For months, Laura had been either lying in bed or sitting in her wheelchair, hours on end, isolated and alone, except for the times we were with her. The more aware she became, the more frustrated she became, and ever so much more homesick. She kept telling people that she could not hear, but the medical staff continued to treat her as if she did. "I know she hears me," said one of the nurses at the hospital.

"Trust us," we said. "She doesn't understand what you are saying. She is picking up on your visual cues."

We didn't know why Laura couldn't hear. Were the sounds not reaching her brain or was her brain interpreting these sounds like a scrambled television channel? There would be tests. In the meantime, we spent hours with her each day writing notes to her and getting her to respond. It was heartbreaking to see our daughter who, only a short time before, had been the center of attention at any gathering, now isolated in a world of muffled silence, unable to use her arms or her legs for any meaningful purpose, or to speak in sentences using more than a few words at a time. She had entered the lonely world of the deaf. The time we spent with her was no longer to console our grief; it was to console hers. I was determined more than ever to get her back.

In mid February, Laura was transferred to Lakeside Rehabilitation Center. There was a hint of spring in the air and we all looked forward to the change. There would be more therapy, we were told, and more of an opportunity to interact with other people. I wasn't convinced. Like all institutions, it can boast a good program, but the proof is in the pudding, and its success depends on the quality of care that she will receive from those with whom she has the most contact. It is the same in any public institution, service organization, or business. Hospitals can have the best programs, the most modern facilities, and the best-trained staff, but if they don't take time to show love and compassion for those they serve, their rhetoric is meaningless. I call it the *Law of the Least Common Denominator*. The quality of care in any institution or place of business is usually reduced to the level of the least caring individual and is often inversely proportional to the salary of the highest paid individual, though not always. When we left Sacred Hands, I gave the following letter to the social worker to read to the staff:

To: All of the Staff at Sacred Hands Rehabilitation Center

+ who helped with Laura's rehabilitation
+ who worked to strengthen her muscles that she has not used for any meaningful purpose since the night of her accident in October
+ who helped her to reconnect with things that were familiar
+ who treated her with dignity and respect and saw to it that she was clean, her hair was washed, and she was presentable to her friends
+ who knew that she could not hear and took the time to write things down on paper so that she would understand what you were saying and not feel so lonely and isolated in her quiet world
+ who showed compassion and support to our family and took the time to express words of encouragement at times when there was very little progress and we needed it the most
+ who took the time to get to know Laura, her thoughts and her feelings, what made her happy and what made her afraid
+ who didn't take for granted their abilities to walk, talk, hear, or use their arms and legs, and used those abilities to help Laura recover hers
+ who for one moment tried to imagine what it has been like for our family these past four months and did not take offense at our frustrations, we are especially grateful.

(There were a few, very few.)

A few months later, I discovered an e-mail that Jaime had written to his dad. It was dated January 21, three months after Laura's accident.

> *I got there last night @ 7:30. She was sitting in the community room facing the nurse's desk. They had her in her white and yellow "straightjacket" strapped down to the chair. Between her vest and the lateral rests, which were pressing into her rib cage, she was strapped in so tight, she could not move any part of her body from her neck down to her knees. She was awake, but had her eyes closed with her chin resting on her chest. It was one of the most disturbing visages that I have ever seen!*
>
> *I walked up to her and took her hand and said, "Hello, Laura." She opened her eyes and her face lit up like a Christmas tree. She said, "Jaime." She had a smile tattooed on her face the whole time I was there. I took her back to the room and unstrapped her and took off her leg rests so she could move around. We talked and goofed around, and I combed her hair in front of the mirror. She said, "My hair is short," very clearly. Then later she said, "I am tired." So I put her into bed. We goofed around with her cage for a little while, and then she fell asleep holding my hand.*
>
> *The night staff has very much of a zookeeper attitude toward patients: make sure the animals are fed and their cages are clean, but don't tease them because they might bite.*

It was not unusual to find Laura like this. On one occasion, the nurses had strapped a thick cloth mitten around her hand.

They were afraid they might be scratched by her beautiful long nails as she reached spastically for human touch. I discovered, like Jesus when confronting the moneychangers in the Temple, that there is a time and place for anger. But I, in my grief, could only feel an overwhelming sense of sadness.

Laura did not want to go to Lakeside. She wanted to go home. We tried to explain to her that Lakeside was where she was going to learn how to walk. She understood for a moment, but her short-term memory loss would cause her to ask again and again. We spent the evening with her, and when it was time to leave, I asked her what she would like us to bring to her the next day. She looked at Jerry and Justin and me and then said, "You, you, and you." Jaime took off work the next day and spent the entire day with her to help her adjust.

Before arriving at Lakeside, we had taken Laura back to Froedtert to see an otolaryngologist and an audiologist for further tests on her hearing. The results indicated that although the hearing mechanism from the outer ear to the cochlea was intact, Laura was effectively deaf. The auditory cortex of her brain did not receive a single sound. We were told that she could stand next to a jet airplane and still not hear it. There was no longer any doubt. Our focus now was to find a way for her to communicate with the world she so desperately missed.

By mid February, our entire family was sick. Justin had missed several days of school, and although we managed to keep him involved in activities, his needs were not being met. None of ours were. I tried to explain to him that this is just something families do when someone is hurting like Laura, but he was hurting, too. Jerry was beyond stressed. He had just returned from Eau Claire in a blizzard, where he had gone to be with Grandma May while she had open-heart surgery. That was something that could be fixed. She was eighty-four, and I guess Heaven just wasn't ready for her yet. When Jerry returned home, he asked me if I had missed him, and I said, "Yes." Then he asked me if I was afraid, and I said, "No. I'm not afraid of anything anymore." Who was it that said in *Lord of the Flies*, "The only way to deal with fear is to confront it."? My worst fears are all around me, and I cannot move in any direction without confronting them.

If ever we needed Laura, it was now. She was the only one who could handle Grandma May. The last time they were together was shortly before the accident, at Uncle Mark's farm just outside of Madison. I remember Grandma May asking Laura why she wasn't wearing the ring that she had given to her. "Don't you like it?" she asked.

"Oh, Grandma, I love it," she said. "In fact, I'm giving a speech on it next week. It's one of my favorite things." Laura had told me about the speech. Everyone else had already given his. One student told about a teddy bear that had been given to him because he had childhood cancer. Another held a picture of his family, the only one he had with both of his parents together before they were divorced.

"What can I talk about? I've never had anything bad ever happen to me," she had asked. I told her that her gift was to make people happy, not sad. She should share that gift with others and not be embarrassed by it. What a wonderful thing it is to be able to bring happiness into the lives of others, especially those who have not had much. After all, she could melt an igloo with her heart if someone needed her to.

That evening, Jerry and I followed her back to Whitewater. I rode in her car while she drove. I trusted her driving. We just wanted to make sure that she arrived at school safely, and it gave us a little more time to spend together. A few days later, we received this letter:

*To My Daddy,*

*I've been meaning to write you for a long time, but just haven't had the chance with everything that has been going on. Anyway, I just wanted to say thank you for all that you have done for me. You've helped me out so much—your wisdom, encouragement and, most of all, your support in everything I do. I wouldn't keep trying to be the best I can be if it weren't for you and Mom always backing me up.*

*You have no idea how much it meant to me when you and Mom followed me home from Uncle Mark's. It really meant a lot to know you cared, and it really made me feel like the luckiest girl in the whole world. I don't have very many friends who can say the same about their parents. In fact, the other night when I got off the phone with you, the few people who were in my room stood in awe. They couldn't believe that I could talk to my dad about boys, school, and friends. My friend, who was listening to us talk, said that in all the years she's known her dad she's never once talked to him like you and I do. You are always there for us kids and cheering us on all the way. You're the best dad in the whole world, and without you I wouldn't be where I am today. You're the best and I Love You.*

*XOXO*
*Love always,*
*La*

When I saw Laura again, she was crying. I asked her why, and she said, "Because I am like this." She was living in hell. We were all living in hell. I couldn't see the light at the end of the tunnel. Maybe that's why God invented Heaven—or was it man who invented it, or was it invented at all? I was beginning to doubt myself, my God, and everything in between.

# XIV

If we can perceive it, why can't it be so? After all, don't the moon and the apple observe the same laws of the universe? Aren't we all governed by the same forces whether we perceive them to be spiritual or not? We accept the unknown only when it becomes known, the future only when it becomes the past. Since tomorrow has not been made known to us, then isn't anything possible? We can choose to believe or not to believe. I have been asking why for so long, maybe I should be asking why not.

Our state of consciousness is anywhere and anytime we choose it to be. We seem never to live in the present. It is either too fleeting or too painful. Once we have perceived the present, it has passed; and the past is all that we seem to be able to hang on to, except for our dreams, which are merely visions formed from our past; and those, too, will eventually fade away in time.

What then do we really have to hold on to? Is our existence nothing more than calcium ions surging across neurons like shooting stars across the evening sky? It would be as difficult to hold on to the moment as it would be to capture a beam of light in the night. At one point in my life I seemed to have so many answers. Now, all I have are questions—questions that will never be answered in this lifetime. What sense does it all make? Much less, what difference? The laws of the universe will continue to govern our lives regardless of our awareness or what we perceive them to be.

My mind leaves my body for hours, only to return a second later. How long will it be before Laura recovers? When will she remember? When will she connect her future with her past? When will she go on again with her life? When will we go on again with ours? Each day is like a lifetime—lost. Oh, just to be able to walk across a sandy beach again and hear the waves pounding against the shore or savor a kiss and dream of things to be.

We spend much of our lives pursuing order. Science teaches us how to organize our world through our senses and how to solve problems systematically. From history we learn about cause and effect and how to put events in sequence. Mathematics is the ultimate in teaching us logical reasoning. The more educated we become, the more difficult it is to accept the randomness of events in our universe. Intellectual thought patterns based on reason, however, often inhibit our understanding, and we must resort to faith in order to see beyond our human limitations. How else could the human race move forward? How else could many of us move beyond the today? How else could we explain tragedies that defy any logical explanation or reasoning?

When I saw Laura tonight, she was lying in bed crying. No one seemed to know how long she had been there or who had seen her last. I knew she hadn't been bathed or had her teeth brushed since she had left Sacred Hands, and that had been several days ago. It was dinnertime, and she was supposed to be in the dining room by five, but no one had bothered to get her up. I crawled into bed with her and asked her why she was crying. "Because I can't remember anything," she said. I held her for a while, then took her to dinner. While she ate, I wrote the whole story down again. She would remember for a while, but by tomorrow it would all be forgotten. I will write it down again for her and again until finally she remembers. I gave her my promise.

Before leaving the hospital, I handed the nurse a note to share with the staff. It closed by saying, "Laura is a wonderful person trapped inside a body that doesn't work. Please help her get out." All the way home I prayed, this time for the strength to fight for what she deserved. And what she deserved was far more than what she had been getting. No one should ever have to suffer like this.

The next day, Laura told us that she wished she were dead.

# XV

How can God let bad things happen to good people? If we believe that he is the master micromanager of our lives, how then can we believe that he is a fair and just and loving God? Or are we in control of the decisions which affect our everyday lives through our own free will? If so, what role does God play in each of our lives? Either there's a reason for all of this to have happened or there isn't. Either God is in control of our lives or we are. Can our own free will choose to believe that God is in control? That question puts us at the limits of human logic. Either way, I have chosen to believe that God has the power to heal our daughter.

Human knowledge tries to explain the laws of the universe but defies any understanding of it in the process. The more our minds travel, the farther we find them from the place we want them to be. As Einstein searched for an understanding of the relativity of light to its speed and Hawking explored a dimension of the universe in which a total absence of light draws us further into the realm of the unknown and the unexplainable, we find ourselves, like Adam and Eve in the Garden of Eden, eating from the tree of knowledge only to discover our own limits restrict what we can understand.

As Laura becomes more and more aware of her limitations, she is, like Hawking and Einstein, in search of the truth about what had happened to her. But she is also like Adam and Eve, moving farther and farther from that place in time where the absence of knowledge is bliss. Where is that place we call the Garden of Eden? Is it really a place, or is it a state of mind or a state of being, like the womb or a coma? Or is it where we find ourselves when deep in prayer and where we find peace in what is good and what is pure and what is true?

Then there's the Garden of Ede. That's what we called Grandma Edie's house where I was born and where I often visit in my dreams. If Grandma Edie were here, she'd know what to do. She'd first tell all of the doctors and nurses that what Laura really needs is a good dose of TLC. Then she'd turn to me and say, "You need to have faith and put more trust in God. Where there's a will, there's a way." Then she'd turn to Laura and say, "How about a back rub?" And could she give a back rub! She would turn her fingers into all the animals on Noah's Ark until I swear it would start to rain. I think I missed her more when I was growing up than I do now. I never gave her enough credit for all of the things that she didn't learn in books. I know right now she's probably giving all the angels back rubs, angels who have been watching over Laura when we're not there. It's one of those things we just have to believe—something, I'm sure, not even Einstein or Hawking could explain.

# XVI

*If we would just put as much energy into foresight as we do hindsight, we would have a little more insight into what happiness truly is.*

The secret of happiness is found only when one loses that which makes one truly happy. Most of us will never discover what that is until it's too late. We're usually so busy longing for the future or lamenting the past that we often lose sight of where we are and what we have at the moment. I began to listen to music—every note, every sound—wondering what it would be like not to hear it again. I tried to laugh, wondering if Laura would ever laugh again. And I hugged the people I loved most, knowing that they were the ones who made the moment worth living.

We spend so much time focusing on being happy that we lose our perspective on what truly enriches our lives, and that is to use our God-given talents in the service of others. Happiness is achieved when we see our reflections in the faces of those with whom we have made a difference.

As the days passed, Laura's life was more and more in God's hands. I asked her one night if she prayed, and she said, "No, I can't fold my hands." So we worked on her hands.

Then she asked me where God was. "Right here," I said.

"I hope so," she responded, "because I need him."

Before leaving I told her, "You will remember, you will walk again, and your hair will grow back, too." And then I hung a sign above her bed that read:

> *Believe in God*
> *Believe in yourself*
> *Believe in family and friends*

We want so much to have control over everything we do and over everything that happens to us, but in the end, we have very little control over anything. Yet we worry most over that over which we have no control. How much easier life would be if we would just focus on that which we can control and leave the rest to God. As Gandhi put it, "The most potent incitement of action is prayer." What can we do to help our daughter recover? Over what do we have control? Where do we begin?

I opened the Yellow Pages to the word *deaf* and began to dial. The first call was the hardest. I couldn't believe that the person I was describing was my daughter. Most calls led nowhere, but one call led to a person willing to see Laura and help us find additional resources. I met her at the hospital and she asked to see Laura's medical records. I showed them to her and she began taking copious notes. Finally, I slammed the records shut and shouted, "I've had it with people trying to assess my daughter. What does any of this have to do with her treatment? What is it that you can do for her right now that will help her deal with her situation? If you can't come up with anything, this meeting is over." I stood up and walked back to Laura's room.

The woman said to me on the way out, "I'll be back. I need to be creative."

What I discovered through my phone calls is that we have created in our society an endless system of referring one person to another, and we end up paying a lot of money for it. When we finally do get people on the other end of the line, they are usually more interested in diagnosis than treatment. It seems, too, that the more degrees attached to a person's name, the more impressed they are with what they find.

As Laura's awareness grew, an aura of sadness enveloped her. The emotionless smiles began to disappear. Her eyes watered constantly from pain, yet she could not cry. She began to ask questions about the accident. Who was with her? Where was she going? Where did it happen? She was frustrated that she couldn't walk, that she couldn't feed herself, and that she couldn't hear. But what frustrated her the most was that she couldn't remember. Her memory was the essence of who she was.

One night, Hanns asked Laura what dreams she had, if these had changed, too. She said, "First, a teacher; second, to marry him; third, to wear different clothes; and fourth, to recover." A teacher helps others achieve their dreams. It would take all of us to help Laura achieve hers.

As a teacher, I have been told that children learn when they have been emotionally satisfied. The thoughts will follow. As I watch Laura struggle with her emotions and relearn so many things, I have discovered the opposite to be true. It is not our emotions that determine our thoughts; it is our thoughts that determine our emotions. On a number of occasions, we showed Laura pictures of people that she had met prior to her accident. Her thoughts precipitated her feelings, and she returned to the point in the relationship that she could remember. Although others had moved well beyond that point, Laura was not able to share the same emotions that a common experience had provided for them. To Laura, there was no experience and therefore no emotion. As Laura became more aware of what had happened to her, her emotional responsiveness increased.

I was aware that my pain was also created by my thoughts, and I needed to control them. For months I had been struggling with ways to go on with my life, but I couldn't, not until Laura went on with hers. The *thought* of what happened to her is unbearable. I cannot separate myself from what she was and what she is and what she might become or might have become. Our souls, hers and mine, are attached by an invisible umbilical cord, but the person I see is one I do not know and do not understand. I have tried to create a mental paradigm that would allow such a thing as this to happen, that would force a beautiful young woman to spend the rest of her life in such a wretched state. But there is none. And to continue a *normal* life with her like this is impossible.

I have tried to find words to make sense of it all, from the philosophers whose writings brought order to chaos, and from the poets who wrote of the human condition. But there are no words. No words at all to describe such despair. Sometimes I would hold her and touch her heart and smell her sweetness. And then, she would pull away, so familiar, yet a stranger in my arms. My grief for her was far greater than for me. I had lost a daughter, but she had lost her self.

I have become immobilized by my thoughts. They are as debilitating as the absence of them is to my daughter. If I tell her what she cannot remember, it will release me from remembering what I cannot tell her. Thoughts ... like an atomic bomb, they are so powerful when they radiate outward, only to explode inward, destroying everything I have become.

# XVII

There are those who walk by unnoticed. There are those whose lives simply cross our paths. There are those who point us in a new direction. And there are those with whom we share a common heart.

By spring Laura was spending weekends at home. We had purchased side rails for her bed and adaptive equipment for the bathroom, additional writing boards and dozens and dozens of markers, which the staff at Lakeside used in order to communicate with her. It still took two people to transfer her from one place to another, and Jaime often spent weekends with us to assist with her physical care.

One weekend a friend of mine called to ask how Laura was doing. I said, "She's improving slowly."

She then asked, "How are you doing?"

I said, "The same as Laura. As she improves, so will I."

"But that makes your well-being dependent upon another person," she responded.

"Not just another person," I told her. "My daughter. That's what makes the relationship between a parent and a child so different from any other. From the moment of conception, they become an extension of us. We take pride in their achievements and assume responsibility for their mistakes. That's not just good parenting. It's love—and one of the strongest bonds of love there is."

Laura's friends continued to visit her. Some had changed majors as a result of her accident and had moved away. Others just moved on. A few called with excuses or wrote letters of apology for not seeing her. We understood, but Laura didn't. Love doesn't need excuses. Guilt does.

Laura began to make new friends. Carrie, who had been at Lakeside for over two years, was still breathing through a tracheotomy tube tied around her neck. She had fallen from her bike, and the resulting head injury had caused her to lose her sense of smell and taste, as well as the feelings of fullness and hunger. But she could hear; and she became Laura's ears at the hospital. One day, Carrie and Laura were together in a therapy session when the staff psychologist asked how each person dealt with anger. Laura told the group, "I never tell my mom when I'm angry. I don't want her to worry."

Laura also met Ron. Ron was a state employee who had gone to Lakeside to visit Laura. He had been deaf since birth. His mother had had rubella while she was pregnant with him. His wife was also deaf. They had four children, all of whom were fluent in sign and had to go to school to learn English as their second language. We hoped that, in time, Ron would help Laura connect with the silent world outside of the hospital.

There were others, too, like Amy, a sign language teacher who tried to help Laura discover that there is as much beauty in the sunsets as in the songs of the birds. So many people; so many people giving of their lives and so many people in need of help; people who I never knew to exist, all living incredible lives, overcoming incredible obstacles, in the slow, invisible lane of life.

Hanns spent many hours each weekend visiting Laura, and he managed to steal away from his studies at Whitewater several times each week to be with her during therapy. It was only an hour round-trip to Lakeside from the university compared to the three hour drive that he would make to Sacred Hands in the middle of winter. On one of his visits to see her, Laura asked him, "Does it bother you to see me like this?"

He said, "If it did, I wouldn't be here."

I've often thought about the people that our society holds up as heroes—sports figures, movie stars, and balloonists circumventing the globe—all people pursuing pleasure for personal gain. If my eyes were the lens of a camera, I'd focus instead on the quiet heroes of this world: people like Hanns, who give of themselves out of love, the thankless ones, doing what they do not for money or personal recognition but because it is just the right thing to do. Hanns spent his twentieth birthday with Laura, surrounded by others who were brain injured. Jaime did the same on his twenty-sixth.

On Palm Sunday, we took Laura to church. It was the first time in six months that she had been anywhere except the hospital or home. A young girl stared at her as we wrote notes with dry markers on a portable lap desk and held the hymnal in front of her as if she could hear. I wanted her to holler, "I know that music! I could play it. I've taken piano lessons since I was five, and I've taught flute lessons, too. I can read German and English and was a foreign exchange student and have traveled to other countries and took ballet lessons and jazz, and I was just on a hayride with students from my dorm—" Instead, she just smiled, that blank, emotionless smile, and shook her head and arms uncontrollably. The young girl continued to stare. All I could do was wave my palm and sing, "Hosanna, hosanna in the highest," and smile with her.

# XVIII

Easter came and went. The daffodils bloomed and died. The geese all flew north again and Orion had nearly completed its path across the winter sky. No one can bear another's pain. My pain is not my daughter's; her pain is not mine. I am not sure what Christ's death had to do with the suffering we feel here on earth. It just reminded me of the innocence of it all.

Memories of a new Laura began to replace the old, and I was afraid that I was forgetting the daughter I had reared. It was part of the healing process, but I didn't want to let go of that part of her life or that part of mine. She was so young, so beautiful, so full of love, and so ready to take on the world, like an indigo bunting soaring across the sky, feeling the power of God in its own wings and ready to perch on every spire, now wounded and unable to fly. It has been said that time heals all wounds, but I think time just erases part of the memory of them. Tragedies bring us closer to God but farther from an understanding of him.

Lakeside was one of two neuro-rehabilitation centers in Wisconsin for treating brain injuries. At each of these facilities, there are three levels of care: acute rehab, sub acute rehab, and long-term rehab. Laura was admitted to acute rehab because she required maximum assistance with her daily activities. Moving into the next levels of rehab would depend on her progress in therapy, which was coming along ever so slowly.

Lakeside featured a dining room on the main floor where residents and their families could eat. On the ceiling of the dining room were beautiful chandeliers, and on the tables were red tablecloths with silverware rolled up in white napkins. Along one wall was a salad buffet that included soup and hot bread and was served at no cost to visitors. Between meals it was a very inviting place to eat. During meals it was another story.

Food was served to the residents according to individual protocol, which was determined by the patient's gag reflex and his/her ability to swallow. It was soft, finely chopped, or pureed. Laura was ordered to eat pureed food, although she had never eaten much of it before, not even as a baby. I usually talked one of the girls in the kitchen into making something that looked a little more palatable, and I would cut it into smaller pieces and feed that to her.

It was in the dining room that we came into contact with many of the other residents. In one corner were the children. They were there for various reasons, mostly associated with behavior. In another corner was Grace. She had been at Lakeside for almost ten years. She screamed throughout dinner. Someone said that she had been beaten senseless and raped repeatedly in another facility. Everyone ignored her except the nurse who was assigned to her. We figured she had every reason to scream.

Some residents never made it to the dining room. Across the hall from Laura was a man we called Grandpa. He had fallen from a tree stand during deer hunting season in November. Pictures of him with his grandchildren sitting on his lap or working on his farm were pasted on his door. His wife was always by his bedside, a smile on her face. She was another quiet hero. Buck was in the room next to Laura. He was a truck driver who had been in a coma since anyone could remember. He never seemed to have any visitors. Down the hall was a young boy who never seemed to have any visitors either. He had swallowed some type of cleaning fluid and would probably spend the rest of his life in an institution.

One night, after leaving the dining room, we ventured by Carrie's room. We hadn't seen her for several days. Two nurses were standing next to her bed with oxygen tanks. She didn't look good. She had been having seizures ever since her accident. We prayed that she would make it, too.

Laura was spending weekends at home. We did everything we could to stimulate her brain. We left newspapers on her bed for her to read. Friends brought her magazines, and Jaime and Uncle Mark printed news articles from the Internet. We kept the television on with closed captions for her to follow, and we continually kept her up to date on the news by writing things down on lapboards. But mostly she just wanted to look at pictures—anything from the days that she could not remember.

A neighbor came by every weekend to strengthen and stretch Laura's muscles. It helped with coordination. A speech pathologist worked on her speech, which had become indistinct. The upper palate in Laura's mouth had no gag reflex and was causing her speech to develop a nasal quality. It would become a more serious problem in time. We all worked on teaching her to lip read. And we continued to play Mozart through earphones hoping that the music would stimulate brain cells to reconnect.

Laura was becoming increasingly aware of her appearance. She knew she looked different, but was unable to do anything about it. She was not able to comb her hair or even brush her teeth. We took her to a beautician and had her hair cut and highlighted. We did her nails and bought her new clothes— not the sexy, tight fitting ones that she used to wear, but ones that were two sizes larger, with elastic around the waist so that she could be dressed more easily. We made weekends something for her to look forward to and something enjoyable upon which she could look back. It helped her to adjust to her new life.

Laura relied entirely on visual cues for information, so when she told us that she couldn't see well, we became concerned. We made an appointment with a neuro-ophthalmologist for testing. Laura arrived in her wheelchair with an entourage of people around her. One of the nurses left the examining room in a panic, and I heard her complain to the doctor that there were so many people in the room that there wasn't enough room to examine Laura. The neuro-ophthalmologist arrived with yet another assistant who just had to see what was going on. The doctor turned out to be quite patient and knowledgeable, however. The pupil in Laura's left eye still did not respond to light differential, and the optic nerves appeared to be damaged. He wrote out a prescription for new glasses, and we made an appointment for more testing to see if the damaged nerves affected other areas of Laura's vision.

It seemed that for every problem that was solved, a new one percolated to the top. The fingers in Laura's left hand would not straighten, and it was painful. Another appointment was made, this time to a hand specialist.

Laura had set a goal to be walking by the end of April. We knew that it was unrealistic, but we knew, too, that the first step in achieving one's goals is to set them. We encouraged her wherever possible. It wasn't a lack of strength that was holding her back. It was balance. The ataxia was causing her legs to kick out uncontrollably in front of her and was not allowing for smooth movement of her other muscles. Doctors told us this was an issue she would deal with for the rest of her life.

One weekend, after doing everything we could possibly do for her, we asked, "What is it that you liked best about the weekend?"

She smiled and said, "Hanns. He means the world to me." That was how it should be. She knew she could count on us for the rest.

We worked as a team, our whole family. We always have and always will. Hanns had become part of our team.

# XIX

My whole life I have spent running a race against time—so many things to do, so much to accomplish. Ideas once flowed more quickly than time, and, in my dreams, my feet never touched the ground. Now, the clocks all seem to have slowed down. I wait to fall asleep; I wait for the alarm to ring; I wait for Laura's brain to heal. For Laura, the clock has all but stopped, too. There is no need to make lists, as she sits quietly in her room trying to remember things that she never will. Someday, it will all reconnect in that eternal continuum, when energy disassociates from matter, where there is no beginning and no end and no clocks to mark our passage and guide our way. Somewhere in time, some time in space, it will all be perfect again.

As I lay and think, I wonder if all that has ever been thought has been said. Has all that is important been written? Does the ultimate truth that we have been seeking even exist? Is it out there, and I am too blind to see it or too deaf to hear it? Or is it within all of us, and I am too numb to feel it? Are all the answers in the scriptures, and, if so, what are they really telling us? That there is renewed hope? That the spirit is stronger than the body? That faith, hope, and love are the core of our strength and will sustain us throughout our existence here on earth?

Are we looking for meaning where none exists? If so, why do we even ask these questions? Is life nothing more than a series of shopping trips to satisfy our wants between interludes of satisfying our basic needs? Is life too short to even ponder such questions, or too short not to?

I read once that people who experience tragedy respond in one of three ways. I had to laugh. They obviously have never experienced tragedy. There is no one way, or two ways, or three ways. Each person must forge his own path through uncharted times, picking up pieces of shattered lives, and holding on to hope wherever he can find it. We struggle to find meaning, and the only meaning we find is in the struggle.

To pick out her new glasses, we took Laura to the same place she had been before, hoping to recreate the experience in her mind. Before returning to Lakeside, we stopped home for a quick dinner of lasagna. I told her that one of the neighbors had made it for us. She asked why. I told her that many people had brought food to our house because we were spending so much time at the hospital. They wanted to help. I also told her that her accident was real hard on the whole family. She looked at me and said, "Especially me!"

I suddenly felt ashamed. I couldn't possibly imagine what she must have been going through. Where she has been, not even Dante could have imagined.

All my thoughts, everything I have written. Should I destroy it all—all my memories along with hers? Or should I try to hold on to them so that maybe someday, a long, long time from now, perhaps long after I am gone, Laura might know how much she is truly loved?

# XX

Laura was stuck in time, too. Like quicksand, she was drawn into a quagmire of empty memories; the more she struggled to remember, the more deeply entangled in her own thoughts she became. "Tell me everything," she told us. "I want to know everything that has happened to me."

"Then will you be able to go on with your life?" I asked.

"Yes," she said.

"I hope so," I told her. We held each other tightly, each of us saying a silent prayer that the other could not hear. God did. He had to. We all echoed her same silent prayer.

One morning in April, we received a call from Lakeside. Laura had fallen in the bathroom. They weren't sure if she needed stitches, so they sent her to a local hospital just in case. When I arrived that evening, Laura was sitting in her room alone, reading the posters we had pinned on her wall. When she turned to look at me, I broke down in tears. Her beautiful smile that, only a year before, had been used by the photography studio to sell senior class pictures, was gone. Her eyes were red and strained, her nose swollen, her lips stitched together in a twisted clump of dried blood. "Don't worry," she said to me. "It will heal."

She went on to tell me what happened. A nurse had taken her to the bathroom and had left her there. Laura rang and no one came. She waited a long time, then tried to pull herself back into her wheelchair. She could not walk. She could not even stand. Her arms shook so badly that she could not grab the railing in the bathroom or the arms on her wheelchair. She fell face down on the ceramic floor. How long she had been lying there before anyone found her, I don't know. Nor do I know how anyone could have been so careless of another human being. How much more can an innocent child suffer? There is so much that I just do not know.

# XXI

*If you can meet with Triumph and Disaster ...*
*Or watch the things you gave your life to, broken ...*
*And so hold on when there is nothing in you*
*Except the Will which says to them: Hold On!*
　　　　　　　　　　　　—Rudyard Kipling

I looked for strength everywhere—in these words of Rudyard Kipling and in the arms of those who continued to reach out.

Laura was now spending every weekend with us. Our lives had come to a standstill, and she became the focus of all of our attention. We had worked hard as a family not to let one person's needs dominate over another's; but, for now, we had no other choice if we wanted her to come back to us. The house was always in a state of chaos, but people did not come to see the house, they came to see her.

One weekend, Laura made a card for Hanns. She practiced writing her name with her left hand until it was finally legible. Then she scrawled a note, which read:

Dear Hanns,

Thank you for going through this with me. You
are the best. I love you so much.

Laura

All day Sunday she waited for him. He had told her he would
be there. People came and left. "You are such an inspiration,"
they told her. "You are so positive." But a mother knows what
is in her daughter's heart. She waited in her silent world until it
was time to return to Lakeside. Still, Hanns had not come.

"This is the hardest thing that I have ever gone through," she
said. There was anguish in her eyes, but she could not cry with
tears. That had been taken away from her, too. We wrote words
of encouragement on her lapboard—all that had been told to
us. I realized, as we talked, that we had moved on, just a little,
though just enough to help her move on, too.

In May, Laura was transferred to the CBRF unit at Lakeside.
It was a move toward independence, although she was a long way
from it. Her new room was across from Carrie's. One day she
asked Carrie if she remembered her accident. "No," said Carrie.
"There are large parts of my life that I don't remember. I've
come to accept that. At least we still have a future." Although I
couldn't imagine what it would be.

Laura then asked Carrie about her family. "Do you ever go
home?"

"No, not much. My family doesn't understand my brain
injury," Carrie told her.

It is difficult for anyone to understand. Without family, it
is impossible.

At the end of the spring semester, the students at Whitewater
invited Laura back to the dorm for a picnic. Classes were in
their final week, and the students had hoped that Laura's visit
would bring closure to all that had taken place during the year.

They showed her pictures and a video and passed the writing board around to tell her of their summer plans or offer words of encouragement. But, for Laura, there was no closure, only sad reminders of all that she had missed.

Laura had been looking forward to this picnic. We had taken her shopping the weekend before so that she would have new clothes for the occasion. When we arrived at Lakeside to pick her up, she was sitting in an empty room. All of her belongings had been moved to another floor the day before. Her new clothes were soiled and they needed to be changed. I asked her how long she had been sitting there. "All day," she said.

"Didn't you have any therapy?" I asked.

"No," she said. "I haven't had any therapy in two days."

For two days, Laura had been sitting in an empty room. When we arrived home from Whitewater, there was a message on our answering machine from Lakeside requesting that we sign some papers so that she could be moved to another unit. The next day I requested a complete investigation of the facility on grounds of neglect.

# XXII

Does our pursuit of happiness bring us closer to that which we seek, or does it take us farther away from it?

Justin grew up this year. He became a man on the night of October 23. Jerry took over where I couldn't be. The two of them grew closer as I grew farther from meeting either of their needs. When our church announced that it was holding evening services, I decided to take Justin. I was hoping to find meaning, to find comfort, and to find God. Then one night, it came to me. Maybe God is nothing more than life itself. And maybe Christ is the human embodiment of all that is good. Maybe it is the goodness we seek in others that saves us from the pain we find in ourselves. Maybe He is our hope, our faith, and our tomorrows. And maybe, just maybe, that is all that we really ever need.

One night, Carrie stopped by Laura's room. "Where is Hanns?" she asked.

"He's coming, and I don't have any makeup on," Laura told her.

"You don't need any makeup," Carrie said. "You have a pretty heart."

"That's all I have left," she told Carrie.

And I thought to myself: *That is more than most people will ever have. I wouldn't trade your heart for anyone else's in the world.*

When Hanns arrived that evening, she handed him a note that read, *I love you so much.* Hanns bought her a candy bar. We walked her down the hall, each holding an arm and praying for the same miracle. Then I left them alone to celebrate their fourth anniversary together.

We spent Memorial Day weekend on Washington Island. Laura slept in her own room for the first time since her accident. I unpacked her clothes while Jerry opened the windows. "Can you hear the sound of the waves?" he asked.

"No," she said. "But I can feel them." Then she said, "It all feels like a dream. It doesn't feel real." It didn't to us either. We were living in our home away from home, the dream home that we had built nearly ten years ago. But the reality of all that had happened in the past year had clouded those dreams.

Laura's mind was caught somewhere between the memories of who she had been and the reality of who she was becoming. She remembered playing in the sand with Justin while we cleared the beach of driftwood. She remembered the friends she had made, and that seemed to be almost everyone. She remembered working as a waitress at the Holiday Inn and the summer she took care of an eighty-two year old woman who had suffered a stroke. She remembered when her life was normal, and she could do all of the things that everyone else seemed to be able to do.

On the way back to Lakeside, Laura said to me, "I think there's a reason for everything, a reason that this happened."

"Hopefully, someday, you will find that reason," I said to her. "It's up to you to make something good out of all of this."

"I will," she said.

I hesitated then asked, "Do you really think there is a reason for everything, or do we simply create reason out of randomness?"

"There is," she said. But I wasn't sure that she understood my question.

I wasn't sure, either, whether reason is often confused with order, and if order isn't simply the sum total of all of the random events that have preceded any given moment in time. We can apply logic to a sequence of events, but reason? If everything we *are* is an accumulation of everything we've *done*, then does it matter if we color inside the lines or not? Does the universe exist outside of the lines that we draw or is it made of all of the lines ever drawn whether they fade away or not? For some unknown reason, I thought, the world is just too complex to be meaningless.

"Perhaps you will not find a reason for what happened," I told her, "but you will find meaning."

When I left Laura that night, she thanked me for everything, especially the chocolate shake. I wanted to go home and put an end to it all, but I had promised that I would see her the next day, and I had always told her never to make promises that you couldn't keep.

# XXIII

The school year ended so unlike it had begun. Jaime took the exam to become a certified financial analyst. Justin finished a season of tennis and earned a trophy for being the best marcher in the high school band. And foliage had grown over the spot where Laura's car had struck the tree.

We spent weekends on Washington Island. Laura walked for hours on end in the swimming pool, supporting herself with a floating tube. Justin made every attempt to get her to engage in water play. She had difficulty interacting and showing her emotions. During the previous summers we had spent on the island, she had kept a diary. She wrote about bonfires and sleepovers with Gretchen and the night she danced with Mike Kickbush at the Firemen's Ball. One night, she asked if I would get it for her to read. She had hoped it would help to fit together the missing pieces of her life. She read until late in the night. After she fell asleep, I picked it up and noticed the last line on the page. It read: *Life is fragile. Cherish it.* All along I had been searching for meaning and I found it that night on the pages of my daughter's diary.

Weekdays were spent at Lakeside and taking her to specialists: Marquette Dental School, where she was fitted with a palatal lift to help her speak more clearly; an audiologist for hearing aids, which did not help; a neuro-otolaryngologist, for more brain scans; a dermatologist; a hand specialist; and physicians specializing in movement disorders. All of these visits resulted in more diagnoses, but we continued to hope that it would all lead somewhere.

We celebrated our thirty-first anniversary in mid June. Our children took us out to dinner. Laura could not follow our conversation. She could read lips only if we spoke slowly and directly to her. Instead, she watched people move silently throughout the restaurant. She recognized many of the waitresses, working the summer before returning to Whitewater in the fall. No one recognized her, she said, because her hair was short. On the way back to Lakeside, Laura continued to sit in silence. "What are you thinking?" I asked her.

"All the things I'm missing out on," she responded.

Hanns had seen Laura every week since her accident. Then, in June, he told her that he wanted to break up with her. He said it was because of something that had happened before her accident that she couldn't remember; but he didn't need an excuse. He needed to move on with his life, and all that they shared at that moment were memories. Another chapter in her life closed, and in ours as well. In Hanns' eyes, I had seen hope, a link between what we had known and loved and what still could be. Her body had been broken, her smile, and now her heart. Hanns continued to see her, but it was not the same. Nothing was the same. And all he could say to her was, "I'm sorry, Laura. I'm so sorry."

In some ways, their breakup released her from her past. Laura would meet new people and make new friends. There would be no unspoken ghosts between them. Hanns cried when he left, and as he drove away, I thought back over the four years that they had spent together— the Friday night taco dinners at our house, the proms, and the long conversations on the phone.

I remembered one evening in particular when Hanns drove into our driveway, and to let Laura know that he was in a hurry, he honked the horn several times. Jerry was irate. He stormed out the door and told Hanns, in no uncertain terms, that if he wished to date his daughter, he was to come to the front door and pick her up like a gentleman. Then, I told Laura that if she expected to be treated like a *princess*, she had better make sure that she always acted like one. And she always did.

On Laura's nineteenth birthday, shortly before her accident, the residents in Laura's dorm threw a surprise birthday party for her. On her head, they placed a crown made out of pink construction paper with the word *princess* glittered across the front. They knew she was a princess, too.

Laura learned to use the TTY, a telephone for the deaf. We purchased one for her to use at Lakeside and another for her to use at home. Each time she made a call, she typed a message to a relay operator, who then spoke directly to the person that Laura had called. When the person on the other end of the line wanted to speak with Laura, the relay operator typed a message back and it appeared on a small screen above the keyboard on Laura's TTY. It was important to let the relay operator know when the message was complete, and this was done by either typing or saying GA or *go ahead*. When a person on either end of the line wanted to end the call, he said or typed SK. Phone conversations on the TTY always took a long time, and sometimes people would hang up on Laura not realizing that she was deaf and using a phone system that created a constant stream of delays. She called me late one night. "Hi, Mom," she typed. "Guess who I saw today?" ... Go Ahead ... "Melanie" ...Go Ahead ... "She was driving her own car."

Laura had met Melanie when she first arrived at Lakeside. Melanie was returning home from college for Christmas vacation when her car slid out of control on a slippery freeway, and her head struck the window. She had been in a coma, also. Laura watched her learn to walk and now drive again. It gave her hope, hope in a way that no one else could give her.

Laura also began to use the computer. She typed one letter at a time with the index finger on her left hand. Emotions that she could not express otherwise would appear on the monitor. To Hanns she wrote the following:

*Dearest Hassie,*

> *I don't understand you. I really need you right now, and I don't know how to get you right now. I have never needed you so badly like I do right now in my life. I love you so much it hurts. I am sorry for whatever I did. Can we possibly start things off slow and work our way up? We have been through so much together and this by far is the most. I love you with all my heart and I would do anything for you. Will you ever find it in your heart to forgive me? Please think about it. I will always love you.*
>
> *Love always and forever,*
> *Laura*

# XXIV

*Truth is within us. It takes no rise from outward things, whatever you may believe. This is an inmost center in us all, where truth abides in fullness.*
—Robert Browning

Peace does not come all at once. It comes in moments. I don't think any of us will ever be fully at peace. That is part of the human condition. It is in the struggle to find peace that souls are transformed into spiritual beings.

We all live in three worlds: the inner world, our inner psyche, a very private world hidden from all others and, at times, from ourselves; the outer world, a world manifested into action by our inner thoughts, a world in which we control all that we do; and a universal world, a world beyond our control, a world to which we must say, "Let go and let God."

Prayer connects our three worlds. It refocuses our energies and realigns our spirits on what is good and true and meaningful. When our actions reflect the purity of our hearts and are channeled outward in the direction of universal truth, we are at peace with ourselves and with God. It is when these three worlds are in conflict, when our actions do not reflect our thoughts and our hearts are in turmoil, that we feel discord within and disharmony with all that surrounds us. Prayer connects us individually with those forces that bind us together in a collective spirit. The energies that are transmitted through prayer are powerful, so powerful that they transcend human understanding and can create miracles—and perhaps a miracle was taking place before our very eyes.

Shortly after Laura's accident, I read a letter from a little boy. It asked, "God, when are you coming back to earth again?"

I would like to write him a letter and tell him, "He has. He has been here all along. And if you are very still and listen deep within the quiet places of your heart, you will find Him, too." As it is written in Luke 17: 21: *Behold the kingdom of God is within you.*

# XXV

If the height of a mountain is measured by the depth of the valley which precedes it, then the potential of our actions can be measured by the depth of the emotions that precipitate them. Ten months after Laura's accident, she returned to Whitewater. I don't think the university had seen a student with as many disabilities, but with as much determination, as our daughter. I knew, at that moment, that Laura would go on with her life, that she would turn tragedy into triumph, and that she would continue to be an inspiration to everyone with whom she came into contact.

Every effort was made at Whitewater to help her succeed. She was given physical therapy, speech therapy, van service, access to swimming, tutoring, and a room on first floor with a special entry key that required just the touch of her finger. She required twenty-four hour on-call assistance, which the university did not provide, so we contacted several agencies in Whitewater that would send someone to the dorm to help her with personal care throughout the day. She was assigned one class: *Disabilities in American Society*. A student aide would sit next to her and take notes on a laptop computer. The material could be saved and printed later for her to study. She still was unable to use her hands even to comb her hair or brush her teeth, nor could she walk or hear. It was a long shot. But Laura was willing to take the risk, and so were we.

Ten months before, no one would have dreamed that Laura would be able to return to the university. She did not plateau. Only therapists plateau. Those not limited by textbook diagnoses were willing to give her a chance; those, like our friends and neighbors, who, long after anyone could possibly imagine, continued to offer their services so that we could spend time helping our daughter. I do not know if it was God working in mysterious ways, but I do know that it was the power of God, working through all of those people, that helped Laura get to the point where she was. Now it was up to her. There were others, too, who could have helped, but didn't, and I realized then that Christianity is not what we profess, but what we practice.

Even five years ago, Laura's returning to college would have been an impossible dream. Universities were not set up to handle people with disabilities. In the 1970s, Congress passed Public Law 94-142, later amended to the Education of Handicapped Children Act, which allowed disabled students access to public education at the elementary and high school levels. But universities lagged woefully behind. It was not until 1990, when President Bush signed the Americans With Disabilities Act, that universities, along with all other public institutions, were obliged to remove barriers and to make accommodations for any otherwise qualified persons to fully participate. Laura fell under the protection of this act. I have never been in favor of government regulating our lives. Government cannot solve problems. People do. Yet I couldn't help but feel grateful for all that had been done to help our daughter move on with her life.

Before returning to Whitewater, Laura became involved in a research study at the Medical College of Wisconsin. Central hearing loss associated with brain injury is unusual, and doctors were interested in finding out what caused it. Brain research was still in the infant stage, and Laura's involvement, we were told, was a gift to medical science. Laura underwent a series of MRI scans to determine which area of the brain responded to sound. MRI refers to magnetic resonance imaging. It is a gigantic machine, which creates an electron magnetic field so powerful that it can erase the magnetic strip on a credit card even when it is not in operation. It works by transmitting sound waves to the brain, which stir up the hydrogen protons in the tissues. As the hydrogen protons realign, they release energy, which is picked up by the magnetic field and programmed into a computer. The computer then detects differences in the amount of energy released by various protons and those calculations appear as images on the screen.

Through a series of MRI scans, various sounds were transmitted through Laura's ears to determine which parts of the brain responded to sound and where blockage might be occurring. She could now hear some sounds and not others. She could hear a basketball bouncing, but not a boom box blaring right next to it. She could hear clapping and doors banging, but not voices. She could hear occasional sounds from the piano, which had been stored in her memory from long hours of piano practice as a child, but she could not hear songs. It had been thought that the right side of the brain responded to music and the left side of the brain responded to voices. These sounds are interpreted in yet another area of the brain. Her involvement in this research project, however, proved that our ability to hear, to perceive sounds and interpret them, is not isolated in any one area and is much more complicated than anyone had ever thought.

Since our bodies are composed of 95 percent water, hydrogen protons are everywhere, in the blood stream and in all the tissues. As I watched Laura undergo these scans, I wondered if thinking wasn't simply the release of energy as protons realigned to their original state, and I wondered if someday a machine more powerful that the MRI would not only be able to detect thought patterns, but be able to create them or even transmit them from one person to another. The MRI is to the medical profession what computers were to education thirty years ago. Laura was a medical mystery, and the technology available to help her was still in the early stages of development. I wondered, too, where all of this would eventually lead—and if any of it would ever help Laura hear again.

When an entire thought pattern is activated by a single stimulus, we call it learning. Experience creates patterns of response so that a single stimulus can trigger a network of neurons to react. A chain reaction of words and images, whether conscious or subconscious, is produced in the brain. When the experience has been erased from the brain or the neurological pathways have been interrupted by injury, the response becomes limited or incomplete. On an external level, this is what often happens in classrooms. Continual disruption interferes with stimulation or the stimulation is incomplete because the experience, or neurological network, is incomplete. In the case of brain-injured people, not only are the pathways of sensory input interrupted, but motor output is interrupted as well. In Laura's case, her injury caused spasticity, ataxia, slurred speech, and hearing loss.

"I want to help people who are going through what I've gone through," she said to me one day. We hoped that not only she but others would someday benefit from her involvement in this research. It was a start.

By the time that Laura left Lakeside, she was receiving two hours of physical therapy each day. She had tried medication to help control tibulation, or tremors, in her right side. A cast was made for her left hand to straighten the joints in her fingers, which the brain had caused to tighten. An occupational therapist worked on strengthening her upper body, a speech pathologist helped to improve her lip reading, and a psychologist assisted her in dealing with the depression associated with her disabilities. At the final staffing, an interpreter was present to type notes for her to read, and a social worker, physician, two medical case managers, and a vocational rehabilitation specialist were also present. It had taken a long time to get to this point, where the medical community finally began to take a more active problem-solving approach in response to her needs. Sometimes, I think it was more of a response to us than to her—to our constant monitoring of personal and medical care, to our insistence upon increased therapy, to our persistent questioning and unwillingness to accept the *wait and see policies* of most professionals in the field of brain injury. We would not be satisfied until we knew that everything possible had been done to help our daughter return to a more normal life.

As Laura left Lakeside, another phase of her life had come to an end. Yet another was about to begin.

# XXVI

We understand life by looking back; we enjoy life by looking forward. Laura had as much to look forward to as we had to look back upon. Perhaps that is why, as we age, we become more cynical—more insightful, but less hopeful. Time becomes a battle between time no longer, except what our minds have done with it, and time ahead, as we perceive it to be. All we have of our past is what we have made of it; and all we have of our future is what we dream it to be. As we age, the battle between dreams and memories intensifies, and who we are depends entirely on which one wins. The future is what our minds create at the moment. None of us will ever be nineteen again, unless, of course we hold those memories dear, and then we can be nineteen forever.

Reality is somewhere between memory and dreams—in the moment, in the now, wherever we find ourselves to be. Where is Laura, the daughter I knew, the person she thought she had become? Where am I? Where are any of us on this journey through time and space, traveling in dimensions that defy the familiar? Are we simply spiritual beings trapped in bodies over which we have no control? Or are our spiritual beings, our souls, creations of our minds, our self image, our image of God and the extent to which we are able to connect the two? What I have found, I cannot explain, and what I could explain, I can no longer find. There is more comfort in not having to ask questions than in not knowing the answers to questions for which there are no answers. We delight in the concrete, in trinkets, which we think define us, and in labels, which point us in the direction we think we are going. Where are we going? Where have we been? Where am I now? Is reality what we see and hear and taste and smell and touch? Or is it what our brains interpret from those senses that is real? The daughter I see and hear and touch, I do not know; but the daughter I feel, I love and understand. And that's what makes it all worthwhile. Thank God for football games, blueberry muffins, and empty gas tanks. It's what keeps our feet grounded and makes it all seem real.

"You will rise to the occasion!" echoed over and over in my mind. "How?" I asked myself again and again. "How will I ever get through this?" Then it came to me, on a beautiful sunny day in August when I would rather have been doing almost anything but what I was doing. It was as if the sky had opened and I was finally able to look up again. If principle takes precedence over self—self image, self-indulgence—then we not only rise *to* the occasion, we rise *above* it. When our actions serve a greater good than those that serve only ourselves, then we can meet with any challenge that confronts us. And those who meet the greatest challenge will serve the greatest good.

That same night, we were invited to the Rodee's. Laura had babysat for their four children the summer before. They took us on a boat ride, which lasted until late in the evening. I listened intently as they told stories of how Laura was the best babysitter they ever had, that she was the only one who could get their children to read and do chores, and how they would do anything for her because she had such a wonderful attitude. They told us why they had hired her. "Because she's a Christian," they said. They told us about praying with her before her accident, and after, and about the time that someone at Sacred Hands had said that she wasn't progressing enough to stay and that she might have to be moved into a nursing home. They told us about going to the hospital with prayer partners who prayed with them, and how a week later, Laura had made considerable improvement and was allowed to stay in the program. They told us how they had been in a business conference at Whitewater and that Laura's name had been brought up in the middle of a conversation because she had touched the lives of so many people on campus. And they told us how they thought God had a plan for her life because her spirit is so strong and there is so much yet for her to do.

I told them how we had prayed the night at the hospital and how her body had quivered, as if life was being poured back into it, and about the times when the streetlights went out after we visited her. I told them about the night that I drove down Lincoln Memorial Drive in the dark, and about the night at Froedtert, after her MRI, when we had driven three cars into the parking lot and above us three streetlights suddenly went out. "It sounds crazy," I said. And just as I said that, the light along the side of the canal that we passed in our boat went out. "See," I said. "It happens all the time."

"It's her energy," they responded. "She is so strong. You can feel it just being with her, even now." Maybe it is just a coincidence, I thought. Then again, maybe there are energy forces beyond our five senses, and I prayed to be part of them.

I knew deep down that it was all just a coincidence, like everything else that had happened. I knew that streetlights are made of vaporized sodium atoms and that periodically they go out to regenerate. I knew that there was an explanation for most of what we experience. But what about the energy that cannot be explained in terms of ions or amps or BTUs, the energy of our spirits, our souls? We can explain so much of what we fear, but we fear so much of what we cannot explain.

# XXVII

The nervous system is very simple. It is based on sensory input and motor output. The brain lies between these two pathways, like a city between two major freeway arteries. The brain not only interprets what our senses perceive, it analyzes, records, processes, synthesizes, and sometimes distorts the messages coming in and the messages going out. What we know about the brain, how it works, how it creates meaningful experience out of what it sees and hears and smells and tastes and touches, is actually very little. And what we do know has led us down the dim side streets of dead-end roads. A year of doctor appointments had led nowhere.

When we left Laura at Whitewater, less than a year after her accident, it was with more reservations than anticipation. Her room was arranged in a similar way to her first dorm room; a TTY had replaced her speakerphone, and a wheelchair was where her futon had been. We tucked a vibrator alarm under her pillow and set the television mode on caption so she could keep up with the news. Above her desk was a letter different than the one I had sent her when she first went off to college. It focused not so much on *becoming* but on *being*:

*Dear Laura,*

> *Touch the lives of all with whom you come into contact, and make the world a better place because you were here.*

*Love ya always,*
*Mom*

Laura returned a different person, and yet, as she said, she was the same inside. A psychologist who had been working with her said that it was his responsibility to help Laura accept her disabilities. Somehow, I don't think anyone has that right. We all have disabilities of one kind or another. If we accept them, what motivation is there to change them? "There are lots of people who go to school and get jobs and go down the aisle in wheelchairs," the psychologist said.

"Not me," Laura told him. "I'm going to walk down the aisle and into my own classroom." I knew that Laura was determined. I knew, too, that it would take a long, long time. Many years would pass, many years of struggle ... and silence.

# XVIII

It was a beautiful fall. The nights were getting colder and the leaves were turning the color of dried blood. It had been nearly a year since Laura's accident. Jerry took Justin to the island for the weekend. He called when he arrived, and I was on the other line with Laura. Since she could only use one finger to type, and there was always a delay in the relay, we could usually have several conversations going on at once.

"It's beautiful up here. I'm sitting on the deck. The sun is filtering through the trees and the hues of Lake Michigan are changing by the minute. What are you doing?" he asked.

"Not much," I said. I was trying to decide which clothes to keep and which to return. I had been shopping that evening and knew that I had purchased too much. Clothes had become like gauze on a wound, and, at that moment, I just couldn't seem to get enough to stop the bleeding.

Jerry picked up on the tone of my voice. "Now what do you have to be down about on a gorgeous day like today?"

If there was anyone that I didn't have to explain anything to, it should have been he. "I'm still having a hard time dealing with all this," I said.

"Well, you just have to," he said. "I guess that's just the cross you'll have to bear."

My mind drifted for a moment to the image of the cross. We all seem to carry one, I thought. It's just that for some people, it is so light that it can be worn on a chain around their necks, a visual symbol of their seeming connectedness, while others bear theirs in heavy silence, withdrawn from the weight of their own suffering. I thought, too, of Christ, of the weight of his cross, and the suffering that he endured, which has lasted for centuries. And I thought of Easter and the innocence of it all. The meaning of the cross was becoming real. It is a symbol of all that must be endured in life, and it can be as light or as heavy as we make it.

"Good-bye, Mom," I heard Laura say on the other line ... GA ...

"Goodbye, honey," I responded ... GA ...

"I love you," ... GA ...

"Love you and miss you, too," ... GA to SK ... *more than you'll ever know!*

As I watched Laura go on with her life, I realized that dreams are more than just wishful thinking. They form the foundation of how we plan to live our lives, a sort of moral blueprint, shaped by the faith, hope, and love of all with whom we come into contact. There are so many people who grow old, not up, and so aimlessly, without vision, without purpose, without hope. They wander through life reacting to the events of their lives. Laura had become the fulfillment of our vision, what we had created as parents, tempered by her own dreams and the vision that she was beginning to form for her own life, a vision that had changed dramatically since her accident.

# XXIX

Laura met Marylee the first week back at Whitewater. Marylee was an artist, a graphic artist, although she dabbled in oils and acrylics as well. Marylee had no arms or legs. She was born that way and had spent the past twenty-six years adjusting to it. She didn't know any other way. She had no idea how or why she was like that. Her mother never discussed it with her. I suspect that she was the victim of thalidomide, a drug women took during pregnancy in the seventies to stop spontaneous abortions. What inspired Laura more than anything else, however, was the fact that Marylee had a boyfriend. Laura had asked a friend once why anyone would ever date someone in a wheelchair. Marylee gave her the answer.

Laura also met Mike. Mike was a physical therapist on campus. He told Laura that he had helped people with ataxia learn to walk. That's all the encouragement she needed. At Lakeside she had been told that she might never walk again. At one point, the physical therapists stopped walking her and worked only on transferring her from the wheelchair to her bed. One night, not long before her dismissal from Lakeside, one of the staff members approached me. "You know you're not supposed to help Laura walk anymore," she said.

I turned to her in utter surprise. "What? You must be kidding. We've been helping her walk every day since she was admitted to Lakeside and before that at Sacred Hands. You know we're going to continue until she can walk on her own."

"If you do," said the nurse, "I'll have to put you on report."

"Well, then," I said, "make sure you spell our names right."

It's unfathomable—rehabilitation facilities that refuse to rehabilitate. It was all part of the nightmare. Facilities which cost in excess of a thousand dollars a day and lack even basic equipment to wash hair, or hire attendants who treat patients with no more respect than if they were lepers. I knew there would come a time when I would have to speak out, when I would have to stand up for those who had been cast aside, when I would become a voice for change. I knew that in my search for God, I was really seeking peace and comfort, and instead, I was given a job to do, a job with no instructions and no guarantee of success. Someday, with the help of God, I would help others who had suffered brain injuries. But for now, I needed to help Laura.

That fall, Laura celebrated her golden birthday. We held an open house in her honor and invited neighbors and friends who had helped her throughout the year. They brought cards and gifts and thoughtful words of encouragement. One card read: "Thank you, Laura. My life is richer for having known you." And another card: "May you have the best birthday ever. You have brought so much happiness to others, you deserve the very best."

I saved these cards, along with all the others, in a box full of memories. As I was putting them away, a note fell onto the floor. It was one that Laura had written to me on my own birthday several years before. It read:

*Dear Mom,*

> *You always told me not to grow up too fast. The truth of the matter is that I want to grow up so that I can be just like you.*
>
> *Love,*
> *Laura*

The truth of the matter is that I had always admired her. She was the one who, in giving of herself, was able to rise above the rest of us.

A week later, I had taken Laura back to Whitewater. It was late and had begun to rain. She started to wheel herself up the ramp to her dorm when her wheelchair became stuck in a puddle. She began to kick her feet to dislodge her wheels. Mud flew all over her khaki pants and her shoes and socks became soaking wet. I stood in the rain and watched my beautiful daughter struggle to be independent and the tears started to roll down my face. Like the rain, they wouldn't stop.

"Why are you crying?" she asked.

"I'm just tired," I responded. I was exhausted.

"No, tell me," she insisted. How could I tell her all that I was feeling? But I didn't need to. She read it in my eyes. "I know I'm different," she said.

"Yes," I said. "But I still love you so very much."

Her swimming coach had canceled that evening and she hadn't had any exercise for two days. "Please take me," she pleaded. So I wiped the tears from my eyes, packed her wheelchair back into the car, and drove to the university pool. As we headed back to the dorm, the streetlights began to flicker and then go out. I set her up for the week and kissed her good-bye. It would be days before the rain would stop, and days before my tears would begin to dry again.

# XXX

The road by our house is one of the most beautiful roads in the country. It winds peacefully through the Kettle Moraine State Forest in southeast Wisconsin. We were one of the first families to settle in the area nearly twenty-five years ago, when old Ted Morey swapped a piece of virgin land with a more open piece that the state wanted to make into a campground.

Ted Morey was proud of the road he designed. He spent much of his day in his later years traveling throughout the area, stopping occasionally to watch as we hacked away at the large white oaks and marked the spot where we planned to build our home.

Old Ted watched every family settle into our community—the horse ranchers, the llama farmers, and those just fleeing the city for the tranquility of rural life. One could set his watch by Old Ted's daily routine, and I was convinced that one could walk faster than he ever drove. Finally, Ted stopped coming, and we began to watch. We watched people come and go. Those who relished the privacy of the area stayed, and those who despised the isolation left.

A day seldom passed that we didn't take an evening walk on our road. Shortly after dusk, Jerry would holler at me, "Marily, come out here. You can see the evening glow." It was that time in the spectrum of the setting sun, somewhere between the descending blues and reds, when everything seemed to emit a warmth of its own. It was a peaceful time. In the spring, we'd pass by Juchem's pond and hear the peepers. That was what we called the young frogs, and it was always a sign of new life to come. In the summer, we'd walk to the top of Hall's hill. That was where Jerry taught all of us to read the sky. In the fall, we'd hear the katydids screech their warning for a cold winter ahead, and we'd watch the leaves change color before our eyes. And in the winter, we would talk. Sometimes we talked about the days that had passed, and sometimes we talked about the days to come.

We knew everyone on our road. I remember the first time we met Florence and David. They were standing on the side of the road studying the spot where they, too, would build their dream home. Suddenly, out from the woods bounded the largest dog I had ever seen. I thought at first it was a bear and grabbed Jaime, who was running toward me thinking the same thing. It was their Newfoundland, and years later, when it was near death, I recall Jerry running down the road to help Florence put it in the car to take it to the vet, but it was too late. Jaime met their son Patrick the same day that we had met Florence and David. They were only three, and they became lifelong friends. When Patrick married and became a minister, Jaime stood up at his wedding. When Jaime married, Patrick was there as well. They both got into more trouble on that road, but they learned lessons, too—lessons that Patrick uses today in his sermons, and Jaime in his daily life.

I've always loved our road. It was where Jaime and Laura and Justin all learned to ride bikes. It was where they waited for the school bus to pick them up in the morning and where I waited for them to come home at night. It was where we picked berries, where the boys could play ball, and where Laura and I would wrap our arms around each other and giggle and talk. It was where Sophie, our dog for all of our children's growing-up years, would bark at the joggers or the bikers who passed by. She always kept an eye on the children, and when they'd venture too far from sight, she was always there to nudge them back to safety.

There was seldom a day that we didn't see some type of animal on our road. There were chipmunks and squirrels and rabbits, opossum, raccoon, and deer. One time Sophie ran head on into a skunk and it sprayed her right in the mouth. It was six months before we could get the smell out of her and out of the house. Another time, she flushed a badger out of the woods and shook its head until it was lifeless. We all stood in the middle of the road, staring in horror and awe.

Other people loved our road, too. Sometimes they would come out from the city and would use our road in the name of some charity, spray painting arrows for others to follow. The spray paint lasted long after those do-gooders, and I'd follow them and ask them if they'd mind if someone spray painted their road. It didn't seem to do any good because each year they'd return. Finally, I went to the town hall and had an ordinance written making it unlawful for any unauthorized person to mark up our road. Jerry calls it Marily's Law, and I have been vigilant in enforcing it ever since.

One night, when Jerry and I were out for a walk, someone drove by in a white car, much too fast for our comfort. Jerry hollered, "Slow down!"

The driver was obviously offended because she turned around and began to holler back. "This is my road, too," she said, and came to a screeching halt in front of us. Her husband pulled alongside on his motorcycle, yanked off his helmet, and started walking toward us. "What's the problem?" he demanded. "You some sort of a cop?"

"No," we said. "We just want your wife to slow down. Our daughter had an accident on this road near the Kettle Moraine Ranch."

"Let's settle this here and now," he shouted, taking a fighter's stance as if to throw a punch.

A lifetime flashed across my mind. I grabbed Jerry's arm and pulled him in the direction of our house. "Let's go," I said. "Some people will just never understand."

# XXXI

It was Saturday night, October 23, one year after the accident, to be exact. It was Homecoming weekend. A full moon lit up the night sky. When I arrived in Whitewater, Laura was sitting alone in her room. Half-filled juice bottles littered the desktop and a pile of laundry spilled over in one corner. She was busy on her TTY. Her attendants hadn't shown up for lunch or dinner. None of her former friends were home. Hanns was on Homecoming court, and he was at the dance. "I saw his new girlfriend," she told me. "It's OK, Mom. I'm completely over him." But her computer screen told a different story. It mirrored what was behind her smile, what she didn't want the rest of the world to know. She had typed an e-mail to Hanns. "Where are you? I thought you said we could still be friends. Do you know what night this is? I need to talk to you." I turned away. I couldn't read anymore.

We went to Wal-Mart and then to dinner. I bought her a new watch, one with an elastic band that she could put on by herself, and a new outfit. "I don't know what I would have done if you hadn't come," she said. "Will you come back tomorrow?"

"Yes," I said.

"Promise?"

"I promise. What are you going to do the rest of the evening?" I asked.

"Oh, maybe just take a nap. Maybe I'll read a little."

"Why don't you come home with us tonight?" I asked her.

"No," she responded. I knew she was hoping that someone would come.

When I left, Laura put on her new sweater and curled up into bed. I returned home. The dresses from all of the previous Homecomings were hung neatly in her bedroom closet. Her room had pictures everywhere, of those special days when she and Hanns would get all dressed up, dine at a fancy restaurant, and then, arms around each other's neck, would dance the night away. Dried flowers dotted the bulletin board near her dresser, and jewelry to match each dress was neatly tucked away inside.

I recall a sermon one Sunday not too long ago about how much time we spend accessorizing our lives. Laura's room was full of accessories, and behind each accessory was a memory, which I cherished. I remember the shopping trips to the mall, the fitting rooms, and the expression on her face when I would say, "Go ahead. Get the one you like. You look gorgeous in it. I'll handle your father." She would grab my hand. She had such beautiful hands. Her fingers were long and slender and her nails … oh, her nails. Jenna confided once that when she was younger she prayed that someday she would have nails as beautiful as Laura's. Laura was often told that she could model her hands. And I was told that she inherited them from her great grandmother, a concert pianist who had studied under Franz Liszt, but had given up an international career in music because she had married. All that was long ago. Now Laura's hands were held close to her body. They could no longer play the piano or the flute or dial the phone or make a piece of toast or write a letter. They no longer reached out to soothe my troubled heart. The muscles had atrophied and her brain had caused the tips of her fingers to curve upward. Her gift of touch, which had touched so many, was strangely quiet.

# XXXII

One Sunday, a woman approached me after church. "How are you doing?" she asked. Her son had been killed by a drunk driver nearly fifteen years ago. He also was a student at Whitewater.

"Oh, fine, I guess. It's just that it's been over a year now and all I think about is my daughter."

"Life goes on," she said.

"I know. But it's just not the same."

"It never will be," she responded. "Give it time."

*Time*, I thought, as relative to one's consciousness as matter is to energy. Our perception of time lies deep within the cerebral cortex of the brain. It's what connects us to the here and now, orienting us not only to time, but to space. Stored within the cerebral cortex are memory cells of other times and other places, that which we call experience, and from these we form our future dreams.

When a person's brain has been injured, he becomes disoriented in time and space, existing as if in the REM stage of a dream. Events become disjointed and out of sequence. A person can lose a sense of the past and the present, which is the basis for our understanding of cause and effect. If the area of the brain responsible for motivation is injured, a person stops dreaming altogether.

This disconnectedness between the cerebral cortex and the deeper, more centralized areas of the brain is in part what causes one to become unconscious or why one can remain in a coma for long periods of time. It is also why those who have been brain injured have difficulty organizing daily activities, and why they have difficulty collaborating, or pulling it all together, not only within themselves, but with others.

*Time*, I thought. We will both need lots of time.

# XXXIII

*What lies behind us and what lies before us are*
*small matters when compared to what lies within*
*us.*

—Ralph Waldo Emerson

The God of time and place, the God of forces and events, the God who can separate the waters of the Red Sea, who can sail comets across the sky, who can shatter lives with the twist of a tornado or the gust of a hurricane, this God we can see, we can feel, we can taste, we can smell, and we can even attempt to understand—but the God of love? We can find this God in the rainbow, but can we find him in the storm that precedes it? Can we find him in the midst of such tragic circumstances that fall upon our lives? If God is love, then is love God? Is God the master of our fate? Or are we the artists and artisans of our own lives, holding the power to mold matter into meaningful experience; and is our circumstance nothing more than the palette upon which we paint our spiritual vision? Is this the science of the soul? Who are we really, when all that has ever mattered pales in retrospect to what we are experiencing from within? Is this where we find God, the God of love—love for all that is life, love for all that is just, and all that just is?

So much of who we are is determined by the circumstances in which we find ourselves. We are who we perceive ourselves to be: a teacher, a lawyer, a student, an artist. What if all of this was taken away, all of our accomplishments, our accolades, our personal treasures and trophies of success? What if everything we had worked for was suddenly gone? Everything that is familiar, that defines us, vanished? Who are we then? Are we merely victims of circumstance or creatures of external forces over which we have no control? If everything has been taken away, all likeness to the physical and emotional beings we had been just moments before, are we still the same person? It is all so relative—and to what? A name? A face? A memory? A dream? Or is it?

When all has been lost, there remains inside of us a freedom to choose—not to choose our circumstance, but to choose our reaction to it. It is expressed in our attitude, but it lies much deeper than that, deep within our soul. It is a power so great within us that we can conquer fear, and we can overcome loss. This power is at the heart of our spiritual being; it is the power of love.

We are born with a spirit but not a spiritual vision. Our spiritual vision develops long before we are born, shaped by every living soul with whom we come into contact. From the point of conception, a mother nurtures her unborn child. If he is conceived in love, he will most likely grow in love. Not long after birth, others contribute to the child's growing spiritual vision. Friends, relatives, teachers, ministers, and people in his everyday life let the child know into what kind of world he has been born. So many parents are concerned about providing their child with everything, but they neglect the quiet places of the heart, the place where a child learns to have faith and hope and love and a belief in a power greater than himself, which will allow him to withstand the circumstances of his life.

Our spiritual vision defines what we do; what we do gives us purpose; and purpose gives life meaning. We are free to choose our spiritual vision and therefore we are free to determine the meaning of the circumstances in which we find ourselves. If our spiritual vision is connected to a power greater than ourselves, then the meaning we draw from life will be greater than the sum of our circumstances.

Not only do we find meaning in purpose, we find purpose in responsibility. Thus, there is meaning in being responsible. Our attitude toward responsibility is what ultimately determines our happiness. When we seek responsibility, we often find happiness, but when we seek happiness, we seldom find meaning and often act irresponsibly. I've seen so many people whose lives seem void of any meaning—young people lashing out in anger at parents, teachers, strangers, vandalizing, attempting suicide, or just dropping out. Adults, glued to television sets or wandering aimlessly from aisle to aisle trying to decide which pick-me-up they can most afford. They seem to live from day to day, seeking only the pleasure of the moment.

So many parents try to make their children happy by buying them things. But happiness cannot be bought. By trying to do so, parents only create overindulgent consumers like themselves, void of purpose or commitment. Each one of us must find our own happiness, in our attitudes toward what we do, and toward the purpose we find in our lives. The greatest gift of love a parent can give a child is discipline—the discipline that enables him to act responsibly, not only toward himself, but toward everyone he encounters.

Dreams create a purpose for our lives. When our dreams are rooted in spiritual vision, our lives have meaning. Meaning is not found in the circumstances in which we find ourselves. It is found in our response to those circumstances. If one's inner core is solid, if one's beliefs serve a purpose greater than oneself, then life becomes merely a stage upon which to act one's part, and the circumstances of the moment become merely a scene in a play that never ends.

All of my life I have found purpose in helping others achieve their potential—first, my family; then, my students; now, Laura. I have taught our children to behave responsibly and have found happiness in all that I've been able to do. But Laura's accident has changed all that. With her, I will need to begin all over again. And yet, if I expect her to become the best that she can be, why should I expect any less of myself? There is meaning in that, too.

The attempt to understand life, however, should never exceed one's passion to live it. What we do is a manifestation of what we believe, regardless of how we define it. We must, in the end, hold on to what is good. Hold on ... hold on ... hold on to life itself.

# XXXIV

Laura met Cory at Whitewater. There was something about her smile, and there was something about the patience in his eyes when she spoke to him. He knew right away what had happened to her. He had been in a car accident, too. He had been in a coma for four days and was still suffering from its effects. That was five years ago.

"A person's brain is like a computer," he told me when I first met him. "When a person has a brain injury, it's as if everything is wiped out and needs to be reprogrammed."

"That might be true," I said. "I just want her back the way she was."

"She never will be. If you expect her to be, you're just setting both of you up for a big fall. She has no way to get there," he said.

"Well," I said. "I'm going to spend the rest of my life trying. I won't ever give up on her."

"Then you don't know much about brain injury," he responded.

Does anyone? I thought. And what right did he have to talk to me like that? Yet I admired his forthrightness and his understanding of her. Laura could talk to him. He accepted her as she was. He was not connected with her past, and he could help her to bridge the gap between the old and the new.

We celebrated Christmas—Laura's second since her accident, her first at being home. The days before were filled with the usual preparation. We had little time at home. Laura had returned to Lakeside for more therapy, and evenings were spent visiting her. Justin practiced Christmas songs on the piano and a few presents were wrapped. I had yet to do any baking and the tree wasn't even purchased, much less up and decorated. At school, students participated in holiday programs and teachers complained about how stressed out they were this time of the year. I thought back to the time in my life when I had equated stress with busyness, and when, at any given moment, I, too, could have walked away from it all.

One afternoon, parents arrived at school to see their children perform in the Christmas concert. One parent brought a corsage for her daughter and asked me to help pin it on her. I could see the pride in the mother's eyes as she focused her energy on her daughter's accomplishments. I thought back to all of the Christmas programs that we had attended for our children, thirty-nine in all. What priceless moments they were.

Another parent arrived. She, too, had come to watch her daughter perform. But her thoughts were on the conference to follow. Her daughter had told her the night before that I didn't approve of the idea for her science fair project. Apparently the child's feelings were hurt and the mother had come to express her outrage. The daughter's performance was soon forgotten as the mother's anger intensified. Again I thought of Laura. The evening before I had taken her to the dentist for a routine cleaning only to discover that the metal brackets made to hold the palatal lift in place had become embedded in her cheek. She had been in constant pain but seldom complained. As the dentist pried the brackets from her teeth and dislodged the metal from her cheeks, I noticed the black and blue marks covering nearly every limb of her body. She had either fallen or had struck something because of her ataxia. I asked her if it hurt. "I'm tough," she had said, and my mind drifted back to the angry mother with the daughter whose feelings were hurt over an idea for a science fair project. I wondered. Where do we put our energies? On what do we spend our time? Where are our priorities? How many opportunities are missed because of anger? And why does it take a tragedy like this to make us realize what is truly important?

Just before Christmas, I picked Laura up at Lakeside to bring her home. On the way to her room, I passed by another patient that I had spoken to before; I knew she had been there a long time. "Merry Christmas," I said to her.

"Merry Christmas," she responded.

"How are you doing today?" I asked.

"I'd be doing better if I were out of here," she said.

"Are you going home soon?" I asked.

"I don't know where home is," she said and stared at me as if I could tell her where to look. There was a story in her eyes—a story that, for whatever reason, could not be told. Home for all of us is more than just a place. It's a *piece* or *peace* of mind. It's that part in our heart where we find comfort and security. It's where all that is pleasant gathers, where all that is good survives. I knew that for some people, home did not exist. But for Laura, it would never be very far away.

As we left Lakeside, Laura said to me, "I told Cory that in five years, I'll be 99 percent the old Laura." He said, "No, Laura. In five years, you'll be 100 percent the new Laura." Cory spent the early part of Christmas Eve with our family. He put his arm around her and her eyes lit up brighter than any light on our tree.

I thought again of what a friend had once said when I told her how much I missed the old Laura. "The new Laura will be special, too," she said. She was right. The new Laura was very special, too.

The Christmas service was beautiful. The choir seemed to sing more sweetly than ever. A flutist accompanied the organist on the old familiar hymns. I closed my eyes to hold back the tears as I pictured Laura with her flute on so many Christmases past. Now she was sitting next to me, staring off into space. "You used to get much of your stimulation through what you heard," I wrote to her. "Now you need to rely on what you see." I felt that she should have been more actively involved in the service.

"I hate the words *used to*," she said, in a voice loud enough that I wasn't the only one to hear. "It makes me feel like you don't accept me the way I am. The old Laura is gone. She is never coming back." Maybe Cory was right. Maybe I didn't understand. How could anyone understand? So much of what we lose we can do without. But to lose one's self, one's identity, one's future dreams, one's memory of the past? How could anyone understand what it would be like to be alive and yet no longer exist, to suddenly wake up and not know who you are or where you came from or where you are going, to exist only in the present, to be alive and yet to be living the death of your self? Then again, maybe I was the only one who really did understand.

# XXXV

We are
but figments of our own imagining
drifting timelessly
like foam upon the crest
of what was once a wave—
no more than the reflection of our soul
and ripples never felt
as we plummet into the deep, dark unknown ...

I cannot leave her now,
not yet;
I must be her hands, her feet, her ears;
Her thoughts—they are her own;
Someday, she will let go
and I will once again feel joy
and live in peace along the water's edge.

Days turned to weeks; weeks, to months; months, to years. We start out writing one story and the events of our lives write another. I long for the days when I would get upset at cupboard doors left open and kids tracking in snow on the just washed kitchen floor. I miss terribly the arguments over who was going to empty the dishwasher and why the light bill was so high and the phone lines always tied up. I would give anything for the days when I had everything and wanted more.

Jenna became a teacher, mostly because of Laura. Mike became an architect and Hanns went on to marry someone else. Justin graduated from high school and then college, and Jaime continued to move up the corporate ladder. Jerry and I both retired, but none of our lives were ever the same.

I watched the relationship between Cory and Laura blossom, then fade like the petals of a spring bouquet. So in love, yet so many dreams shattered and so many promises broken. And I wondered: how many roads do we never travel, how many forks do we never cross, and would a flower be less beautiful if it had bloomed on another branch? I watched Laura redefine her life again and again. "The new Laura is who I am now," she once wrote to a friend, "since the old Laura is still wrapped around a tree."

I couldn't let go of what I had nourished and cherished and so loved. Yet I could not allow the new Laura to replace the old. Somehow, I had to find a place in my heart for both.

For a long time now, I've sought the truth, the divine truth, searching for answers to explain the human condition, trying to find meaning in all that has happened. What I have found instead is that we seek God with our heads, but we find him with our hearts. There is no explanation for any of this, nor will there ever be. No one is born exempt from sorrow. Mourning is as universal as human tragedy itself. It is rising above it that defines the human spirit and distinguishes us from the circumstances in which we find ourselves. It is, in the end, what connects us with the God we are seeking. Just as new life springs from ashes, so does a new life grow out of tragedy, a life that is deeper and richer and more alive than ever before. I long for that day to come.

# XXXVI

*Dearest Mother and Father,*

*Sometimes it's easier to write than talk. More than a year ago in January, I was at Sacred Hands Rehab. Center, and I can remember lying in my cage. I put ALL the energy I had left into somehow clasping my hands together, and I remember praying. I asked God for help. I was a perfect woman; beautiful, loving. I had a serious boy friend, an endless amount of friends, and the list could go on. Then one day, it ALL came to a halt.*

*I'm slowly putting my life back together, but it may take some time. All I ask is for you to be a little patient while I relearn how to live again.*

*Love,*
*Laura*

Our values guide us more than our plans.

Laura stayed at Whitewater for two semesters. But by spring, all the systems that we had set in place the year before had fallen through. Friendships faded, attendants often failed to show, and Laura slowly began to give up on herself. "I cannot go to school and learn to walk at the same time," she said. We still enrolled her in summer school.

"I will be your tutor and your note taker and your attendant," I told her. "Just don't give up, don't ever give up." I didn't know where my thoughts ended and hers began. Her future was my future, and her failures were also mine.

Then the Department of Vocational Rehabilitation (DVR), which had made it possible for her to return to the university, pulled the plug. "She's unemployable," they said. "There is no use training her for a job that doesn't exist. She'll have to leave the university." Within a week, Jerry located a group home near where we worked. There she would receive better care. She would be fed, her clothes would be laundered, and she would receive transportation to therapy at Curative Rehabilitation Center near Froedtert. It all seemed too good to be true, until one weekend, Laura refused to go back.

"They're mean to me there. They walk away from me and slam the door on me and call me names. I can read their lips. I've lost everything," she said. "Now I've even lost my freedom to choose." They weren't treating her as a person. They didn't know her. They only saw her shaking body and heard her speak in a slow, distorted voice. They saw her eyes wander, her right eye no longer able to see. They did not know that behind the silence of her ears was a soul, a soul that could feel, a soul in desperate need of love.

The cruelty. The insensitivity. The reality. "It's not the bureaucracies," I thought. "It's the people who run them."

Our love was our only guide, like a beacon of light shining just ahead, leading us in some new direction in search of a way to help our daughter. It would have been easier to give up, to close our eyes in pity. But without us, Laura had no one. I knew that had we not been there for her, had we not demanded the impossible, Laura might still be back at Lakeside: institutionalized, sedated, and even more alone. We took her to every specialist we could find. No one seemed to have an answer. We tried medication to control the ataxia and painful Botox injections to relieve the spasticity. We did everything we could to exercise her body and stimulate her mind. We enrolled her in a writing class at the technical school and made arrangements for her to swim every day. She was determined, too, and that would carry her a long way.

Laura came home on weekends. As her awareness increased, so did her frustrations. We solicited the help of a psychiatrist. If he could see her, it would diffuse some of the anger with which we'd have to deal. Or so we had hoped. One Friday evening, we returned home to find a message on our answering machine. "Laura has been having difficulty with the staff. I spoke with her about controlling her behavior. She's calling everyone on the TTY. Perhaps you should consider removing it from her room. She wants to go back to college. Her goals are very unrealistic. It will be a long time before she will ever leave the group home. She should learn to accept that." Unrealistic? To have everything that she had lost—to want to be normal again? Where was he coming from? He was supposed to be an expert in brain injury. By Monday, he received the following fax from Jerry:

*Dear Dr.—:*

> *I received your phone message on Friday, and was rather taken aback by it. So thought I would try and respond in writing so you are aware of how we are dealing with Laura's injury and frustration. First, I think you should be aware that Laura was quite disappointed with the Friday visit. I believe*

*that she has seen you as an advocate, someone to help her through this difficult phase of her life. After listening to your message on Friday, I understand why she was so disappointed.*

*When dealing with Laura, I think the most fundamental feeling to bring to her is compassion and empathy. As my wife has stated to many health care professionals, close one eye, plug your ears, shake all over your right side, and take away the ability to walk. Think about that for several minutes and then you will understand her world. And because her head is quite clear now, she fully understands her losses, and is hugely frustrated. From your message on Friday, I don't think you truly understand that. But please think about it. You mentioned several times that Laura's behavioral difficulties were unprovoked. That misses the point. Her behavioral difficulties are a direct result of her deep frustrations that she has every right to feel. You or I would have those same frustrations if we were in her place. That is why a very deep empathy is key to dealing with Laura.*

*In your phone message, you seem to be prescribing a more restrictive environment for Laura (as a way to control behavior). I think that is way off the mark. It is just the opposite of what she needs. Laura does best when she can control her own activities. This issue of independence is extremely important to her, and you need to understand it in order to effectively deal with her needs. You specifically mentioned limiting her phone access. I don't think you realize that the phone and computer are her links to the real world. It would be a huge setback for her to limit them in any way. Aside from the legal implications,* we would be opposed to any such limitations and the attendant behaviors that would follow.

Very specifically, there are three services that we need from you right now that would be a huge contribution to Laura's recovery:

1. To be a sympathetic listener and just let her vent. Her family has a very hard time with this, and it would be a big help if you would fill that role.
2. Help her to accept and adjust to the new person she has become. It is very heartbreaking for her family when she tells us she doesn't like this new person. I believe that any professional that works with her has to help her adjust to this new life (not punish her for it!).
3. Help her to find a new niche in her changed life—something that she can be part of and contribute to. Right now she has very little to look forward to on a day-to-day basis—therapy, swimming, computer, WCTC. This is a very limited life, and she knows it. That is why reaching out to Whitewater with hope and planning is a good thing. She is trying to plan beyond her limitations. Please help her with this! If these are roles that you feel you cannot handle, perhaps we need to find another professional that can fill these critical needs.

And finally, there is another very important role for you to play in all this—with the staff. It is our contention that the group home is quite understaffed to accommodate all the needs that are there—including Laura's. This leads to great frustrations *on their part in dealing with difficult behaviors brought on by brain-injured residents. They need lots of training and assistance in developing that deep empathy I mentioned above. That is where highly trained professionals, such as you, should come in. Laura has made many allegations of mistreatment during her stay there. I would characterize some of them as staff frustrations. After a staffing last fall things got much better. I believe that this needs to be done on an ongoing basis. It seems to me that sometimes the staff is in over its head and needs help. Blaming the residents is not the answer.*

*I hope this lets you know our positions and concerns regarding Laura's difficult road to recovery. We believe she is making progress, albeit slow at this time. She is still grieving her losses and trying to adjust to that new person. I hope you can help her make those adjustments.*

Before I took her back to the group home, Laura turned to me and said, "Mom, promise me something."

"Anything," I said.

"Promise me you'll pray."

"I try," I told her, "but it's getting harder and harder." My prayers no longer had words. If only she had asked me something else.

"I know there's a God," she said. "If you just pray to him, everything will be okay."

"I just wish I could be sure of that."

Then she said to me, "Grandma Edie is okay, too."

"How do you know?" I asked her. "Did you see her?"

"I saw a lot of things when I was in a coma." Her eyes radiated the wisdom of her experience, of one who had lived a lifetime but never will. Wisdom intermingled with fragments of her childhood—an infant, an adolescent, an adult—the one to whom I had given birth—and Grandma Edie, my mother, all over again.

We drove in silence. She could not read my lips in the darkness. "She's living in hell," I thought. And then all the streetlights around me went out.

# XXXVII

Space, time, the speed of light ... Which is relative? Which is constant? Which is God? Are we but three-dimensional beings in a universe that knows no dimensions? Which dimension is life? What is death when one lives long after one has died? Is there a dimension to life that includes death? Or a dimension to death that includes life? Is pain relative to pleasure? Is life relative to death? Is time relative to God? And is God all that is constant?

The more I question, the less I understand. Mathematically, it is all the same—time; space; and the speed of light, our fastest known measurement of time and space. Laura before her accident and after ... Where did she go? Not alive. Not dead. Existing in a dimension of immeasurable unreality, unexplainable in human terms. Perhaps God is that dimension. Perhaps that dimension is God. Is knowledge what keeps us ignorant of God? Must we go to the Garden of Gethsemane to find Him? Or are we, like ants underfoot, incapable of understanding the magnitude of a power beyond the dimensions of our own reality? Must we know God to know that he exists?

I fear my questions only lead me further from the truth. Time, space, and the speed of light—the dimensions that we define as life. Space and time are relative to the speed of light and all are relative to our existence. They are all measurements, which we have created to prove our existence, which are relative to our existence, and which, therefore, prove nothing. God is the dimension not relative to time, space, or the speed of light. It is the only dimension that is constant, the dimension not relative to our existence. It is through prayer that we seek to connect with that which is constant, with that which is absolute, with that which we call God. And it is prayer that allows us to transcend the limits of our own existence, of time, space, and the speed of light. Einstein was right, but only to a point. He attempted to prove only that which could be proven, none of which will ever explain my daughter's accident. Coma is life and death. It is a dimension that transcends our own existence.

I pray now to connect with that which I don't understand.

# XXXVIII

If you hold a butterfly
too tight
you crush its wings
and so
I let go
and it flew away
and I sat there
all alone
to ponder
what I had lost.

I lay back, my mind pulsating like a kaleidoscope, white lights flashing toward me, encircled in red. And then there was darkness. I opened my eyes and looked at the clock. How much time had really passed? Hours, days, years? All relative to our state of consciousness. Thoughts—the bridge between the conscious and unconscious, transcending the known into the unknown. Thoughts transcend time, and time can be what one thinks—now, what was, and forever. I dream of what could have been, what is, and what will never be, all at once, as if it were yesterday and tomorrow, before the tree and after, her life and ours, changed in time that cannot be measured but will take a lifetime to endure. Many in their lives will know sadness, but few, such despair. Must we know despair to become wise, and must we become wise to find peace?

Laura began to reach out to the people she had known before her accident. It was something that she had done so easily before, and now it was such a struggle. Cards, letters, e-mails, and phone calls on her TTY—each word typed a letter at a time. But few responded. *Go ahead,* I thought. *Spend your time shopping for pretty clothes. Go to parties and pursue your dreams. And don't look back on those who need you most.*

"I feel like I'm in a prison," she'd say to me, "locked up inside my own body."

She didn't seem to fit in anywhere. Not with the deaf because she was disabled, and not with the disabled because she was deaf. Most brain-injured people do not relate well to each other. They want more than anything to be normal and to live in a normal world. But normal people are just too wrapped up in things that don't really matter to ever understand.

"If only I had the key," I thought. "I would unlock her from herself. And then we'd all be free."

# XXXIX

Closure never comes for some. But nature has its way of surviving and time allows us to move on with our lives. The power of love enables us to overcome great obstacles with dignity and grace, to turn tragedy into triumph, and to create purpose in the existence of each one of us. The spirit is indeed greater than the flesh. The soul will triumph over the most difficult of circumstances.

A friend called one night. "Do you know what the name 'Laura' means?"

"No," I said.

"It means *victor*," she responded. "It wasn't a coincidence that that is what you named your daughter."

I remember sitting in a small, quiet chapel at Froedtert a few days after Laura's accident. A psychologist from the hospital entered and sat down next to me. "I can't deal with this," I said. "Everything I've ever encountered in my life I've been able to work through in a matter of days."

"What are you afraid of," he asked, "that you won't love her anymore?" I didn't understand his question. Why would he ask such a thing? Didn't he understand? Of course I would love her. I will always love her. But that question has haunted me ever since. And in my darkest moments I repeat the answer that I gave him that day in the chapel, over and over to myself. As God was my witness, I promised Laura my love. It was not the kind of love that we associate with passion, but rather a love that required a passionate commitment toward helping another human being. As the changes in Laura became more and more evident, I held on to that love. We all did, as we helped her, day after day, hour after hour, work through her physical, emotional, and spiritual trauma.

I saw that kind of love transformed into action as I watched Jaime sit by her side at Froedtert and Sacred Hands and Lakeside. I heard the outrage in his voice when the medical profession became more consumed with its own expertise than with helping Laura. I could see the patience in his eyes as he walked her up and down the corridors of understaffed institutions, passing room after room of sad neglect, to help his sister learn to walk again. And I saw that kind of love in Justin as I watched him fall asleep night after night staring helplessly at a picture of his older sister whom he adored, only to hold her the next day and try and make her laugh again. He has lived a lifetime, too, and has grown in ways that few people ever will. But I especially saw that kind of love in my husband. His focus on what was important and necessary, his perseverance in getting the best medical care possible for our daughter, his compassion as he listened and spoke to her, and his understanding of the importance of holding our family together, in spite of all that has happened. The love that we had for our daughter was so strong that we would have given our own lives, if only she could have hers back again. Since those quiet moments in the chapel at Froedtert—what seems like an eternity ago—I have learned that our actions without prayer are merely unguided footsteps through life; but prayer without action and without a deep, unbinding, and committed love to sustain it, is only wishful thinking.

Three years after her accident, Laura once again returned to the university. She wants to become a teacher for children with special needs. "Every child deserves a chance," she said. "I want to help give someone else that chance." I don't know how long she will stay or whether or not she will ever get her degree. Her determination has allowed her to surpass the expectations of all but her family. Until our death, we will continue to live her life, one day at a time, struggle by struggle, hoping that someday she will once again find her place in this world.

# XL

When Laura was a little girl, I used to tell her the story of the oyster. When the oyster fed on the bottom of the sea, it sometimes swallowed tiny grains of sand. Most of the time, the oyster spit these tiny grains of sand back into the sea. But sometimes, these grains of sand got stuck in the oyster's tender flesh. This caused the oyster great pain, but the oyster always knew what to do. It surrounded the grain of sand with a milky white substance from within, smoothing its edges so that it no longer caused harm to the oyster. In time, the secretions increased, and the tiny little grain of sand seemed to disappear. In its place was a beautiful white pearl.

Someday, I will tell Laura the story of the young oyster who accidentally swallowed a very large stone. It was so large that the young oyster did not have enough of its own milky secretions to cover it, and it started to die. All of the other oysters were heartbroken. But they knew what to do. They all gathered together and gave the young oyster a little bit of their own secretions until the stone was fully covered in milky white. And in time, the young oyster made the largest pearl the world has ever seen.

So much of what we experience in life is like tiny grains of sand. It's not what happens to us that makes us who we are. It's how we react to it. As for my daughter, Laura, she has become that beautiful pearl.

Much of this journal was written during the night, when it was quiet and I couldn't sleep, and no one would listen but God. It is a private and personal journal, and I share it only because it might help others cope with tragedy in whatever form that might take. If this is read by those who treat brain injured people, so that they might be more understanding and compassionate; or by mothers, so that they stop being so busy with their own lives to cherish those precious and fleeting moments they have with their children; or by daughters, so that they might realize, before it is too late, how much they are truly loved by their parents; then, it will have been worth sharing.

It has been a long time since Laura's accident. She will live many years after I am gone. I don't know if she'll ever achieve my dreams or ever want to. All I can hope for now is that she achieves hers. Every year, over a million people in the United States suffer a brain injury. Many die within two weeks of impact. Even more spend their lives quietly hidden behind institutional walls. A few recover and struggle continuously to overcome difficulties and compensate for deficits. We hear about accidents all of the time on the news. Statistics have become background noise to our busy lives. But behind every statistic is a story; behind every story, a heartache; and behind every heartache is hope. And without hope, there can be no healing.

Most of us, at some time or another, will experience some kind of loss in our lives. When we don't think that we can go on any longer, we do. We struggle each day to move beyond the *ifs* and the *whys* because they only take us back to a point of immeasurable pain. We try to return once again to the security of insecure comforts and material pleasures with the same satisfaction as before, only to discover their value diminishes in the presence of a smile, a kind word, or a beautiful sunset. We learn to enjoy the moment because all there ever really is, is what we have right now. And when we don't think we have any more to give, it's because we haven't reached deep enough inside of ourselves. I don't know that we are any better for having experienced tragedy—certainly wiser in some ways, yet more vulnerable in others.

If anyone can go on with her life in spite of all that has happened to her, it is my daughter Laura. It is her strength, her energy, her heart, her kindness, her love for people, for life and for God that is an inspiration to us all. This is a story about her, but it is my story. Someday, Laura will write her own.

*amen*

*Dear Laura,*

*I began this journal with a letter from you. It is one of my most treasured possessions. Now I would like to end it with a letter from me.*

*At the time of your accident, I thought that both of our worlds had come to an end. I began to write, hoping it would help to make sense out of something that just didn't make any sense at all. As you became more and more aware of what had happened to you, I realized that what I had written would answer some of the questions you have been asking and that someday you would want to know the whole story.*

*As I watched other families struggle with similar situations, I began to see the need for more research into and understanding of brain injury and the need for more compassion in the care of those who have suffered it. Maybe someday, with your permission, this journal could be shared with others who have suffered so that they might know that they are not alone.*

*Shortly after your accident, I was telling someone all about you—your tremendous talents and abilities and your warm and loving personality. I have often said, "Of all the women I have known, I have admired Laura the most." My friend turned to me and said, "It sounds as if anyone can overcome this, it's your daughter." I know that's true. If anyone can turn tragedy into triumph, it is you. We can't always control what happens to us. But we can control how we respond to our circumstances. Make good of all of this. Follow your heart. Be true to yourself and all that you have been taught then pass it on to others in need of your love. Continue to be an inspiration to everyone you meet.*

*Someday, a long time from now, when you have gone on with your life and I no longer have mine, you will look back on this period, and it, too, will seem like nothing more than a moment in time. Remember that I will love you always.*

*From all my heart,*
*Mom*